LE
FRENCH
OVEN

LE
FRENCH
OVEN

HILLARY DAVIS

photographs by STEVEN ROTHFELD

GIBBS SMITH
TO ENRICH AND INSPIRE HUMANKIND

First Edition
19 18   5 4

Published by
Gibbs Smith
P.O. Box 667
Layton, Utah 84041

1.800.835.4993 orders
www.gibbs-smith.com

Designed by Sheryl Dickert
Printed and bound in China

Also by Hillary Davis
French Comfort Food
Cuisine Niçoise: Sun-Kissed Cooking From The French Riviera
A Million A Minute

Gibbs Smith books are printed on either recycled, 100% post-consumer waste, FSC-certified papers or on paper
produced from sustainable PEFC-certified forest/controlled wood source. Learn more at www.pefc.org.

Library of Congress Cataloging-in-Publication Data

Davis, Hillary, 1952-
  Le French oven / Hillary Davis ; photographs by Steven Rothfeld. — First edition.
     pages cm
  Includes index.
  ISBN 978-1-4236-4053-0
1. Dutch oven cooking. I. Rothfeld, Steven. II. Title.

TX840.D88D38 2015
641.5'89—dc23

                    2015008008

CONTENTS

INTRODUCTION

I wandered into my grandmother's kitchen looking for her bright smile, knowing she would have something wonderful for me to taste.

On this day, she had her back to me. She was round and soft and held her waist-long hair in a braid that she wound like a doughnut at the nape of her neck. Now it was unruly, with wisps of hair flying here and there, and as she turned to me I saw that her look was triumphant and her cheeks were flushed. She was pulling a hot pot out of the oven and was swinging it around heavily to land with a thud on the wooden kitchen table. Her pot was bursting at the top with a golden crust that oozed bubbling brown gravy down the sides. Ever since that pot had been brought to her as a gift from Europe, she had not gone a day without using it.

Her coveted pot was an enameled cast iron Dutch oven. If she was the queen of her kitchen, this pot was the queen of her cuisine. She would simmer a beef stew in it, and in the last half hour of cooking, slice in whole sour dill pickles that picked up the scent of beef and flavored the gravy. She would cook a holiday sauerbraten in it. She loved baking fruit in sugar syrup and topping it with dumplings for dessert. She roasted her lamb, basted her chicken, baked her cornbread, and even scrambled eggs in it for our breakfast.

I have it in my kitchen now. The insides are scarred and chipped and almost brown from years of cooking. While I have given her pot a place of honor high on a shelf in my kitchen, mine are all around me, as integral to my way of cooking as hers was for her. The circle has come around. The only difference? I have lots of them. As the years have gone by, I have acquired more and more of them, impervious to logic, rather reveling in discovering a new one or new color or size or vintage piece to add to my collection.

I wish I could talk to my grandmother about it. Times have changed. In those days, she cooked with her one heavy enameled Dutch oven and with her cast iron skillets. She would be amazed that there are so many brands to choose from now, so many sizes, weights, colors, and materials. She would also be fascinated to learn about where they come from and who makes them, as I am. I had no idea that they are handcrafted and one of a kind.

What I did know was that the best are made in France, and those are the ones I collect. It is a subjective and personal opinion based upon years of trying different ones. Mine are French ovens and are 100 percent made in France.

So come join me on this journey to discover the French ovens of France, who creates them, what makes them so special, and why they are the most valuable pot you can have in your kitchen. I have developed recipes for them to show you how versatile they are and to illustrate the many ways they can be used. Try them then come join me at the table. À table!

A Brief History of Dutch Ovens

Cast iron pots molded in sand have been used for centuries and have evolved as different technologies developed, as new manufacturers arrived on the scene, and as tastes changed.

The technology for making cast iron evolved in China centuries ago during the Iron Age. In Europe, the use of cast iron first developed during the fifteenth century in order to make cannons. It later grew to furnish cast iron pots for households for cooking purposes.

By the late 1700s the Dutch were experimenting with and perfecting a way to cast iron cooking pots in dry sand in order to make them smooth. Many believe the term "Dutch oven" comes from this kind of lidded pot originally made in Holland. The English liked them so much they began to import them then eventually brought the manufacturing process back to England to produce them for English households.

Cast iron cooking pots then migrated with English colonists to America and were indispensable to settlers who pioneered on horseback and in wagons from the East coast to the West coast. The pots had short legs so that the traveling settlers could nestle them into wood-stoked campfires.

In the beginning of the twentieth century, cast iron pots and skillets became very popular in America. Brands like Griswold and Wagner Ware were in demand. Lodge is the only American brand remaining that still produces uncoated cast iron cookware in America at its plant in South Pittsburg, Tennessee, which it has been doing since 1896. (Its enameled Dutch ovens, however, are made in China). Today these kinds of ovens, with legs and lids that can hold burning embers, are referred to as Dutch ovens, camping, chuck wagon, or cowboy Dutch ovens, and are used by campers when cooking over wood fires or using charcoal outdoors.

When we bring cast iron cooking pots indoors to be used on the kitchen stove or in the oven, they

are, more often than not, enameled versions, still referred to as "Dutch" ovens. The process for enameling cast iron Dutch ovens—grinding down glass fragments, color pigments, and minerals together until they are a fine powder that is sprayed onto cast iron pots then fired at high temperatures until the glass melts to fuse with the cast iron and turn into a glossy enamel coating—developed in the twentieth century. They are now made all over the world with varying degrees of quality and price.

While we immediately think of heavy enameled cast iron pots when we hear the term Dutch oven, the term refers to any cast iron, enameled cast iron, ceramic, clay, aluminum, clad, or stainless steel pots that have wide bottoms and high sides with a lid that act like mini ovens, capturing and evenly distributing heat.

I think the best are made in France. The reasons I prefer them is that they have the best design and performance for my needs. With each passing year, French manufacturers have poured more money into research and design in order to make their French ovens function at a higher level, at higher heat, with less weight and increased ability to withstand chipping compared to the relatively lower level of manufacturing standards from ovens made in other countries, where quality control is more questionable. The biggest problem I have had with non-French brands is in the quality of the coating, which tends to crack or chip over time, resulting in the oven having to be replaced

And I have to admit, French ovens (known as *cocottes* in France) are hard for me to resist, as they are sublime to look at and handle, each brand expressing its own look with flair.

So I think it is time to give credit where it is due and call Dutch ovens that are made in France *French ovens*. Mine are French ovens, not Dutch ovens made anywhere else to any other standard.

FRENCH OVEN BRANDS

CHASSEUR

Chasseur French ovens are designed, hand-cast in sand molds, and enameled by hand at the Invicta foundry in Donchery in the Ardennes region of northern France. The foundry and enameling plants have been established since 1924 and are just a few miles away from vineyards producing the celebrated bubbles of Champagne.

The ovens have a nostalgic look and the heavy feel of a traditional French oven. At the foundry, after they have been made in sand molds, they are coated with a black enamel coating, which you can see on the rim to protect them from corrosion. Then they are coated with a second final enamel coat with color. Each piece is one of a kind and comes in a variety of exterior colors, including white, petal pink, black, and meringue.

The round French ovens come in sizes ranging from 1 quart (.9 l) to 8.5 quarts (8 l). The oval French ovens come in sizes ranging from 3.1 quarts (2.9 l) to 7.8 quarts (7.4 l).

They can be used on all heat sources, including open fire, induction, electric, gas, radiant, halogen, and in the oven—and are dishwasher safe. The plastic phenolic knobs can be used in oven temperatures up to 428° F (220° C). Their stainless steel knobs are good to all temperatures.

All Chasseur French ovens come with a 10-year warranty against faulty manufacture under normal usage, which does not cover normal wear or aging.

Note: When cooking on an induction stovetop, never use the booster function and never cook on maximum power. Chasseur also recommends that you "wipe the interior surface with kitchen paper [paper towel] which has been dipped in cooking oil, before storing after use to increase the longevity of the product."

EMILE HENRY

In the midst of historic Burgundy in the town of Marcigny resides one of the major manufacturers of ceramics in France, Emile Henry. However, it began on a very small scale. In 1850, its founder, Jacques Henry, was a potter who opened a workshop to take advantage of local clay, crafting dishes and jugs to make a living. His son, Paul, took the business over from his father for almost 30 years, and then passed it on to his son Emile. And so it went until today, passing from father to son, while each generation grew the business until 2012 when sixth-generation Jean-Baptiste Henry took the reigns.

I was very familiar with Emile Henry bakeware and dishes, but until recently, I was not aware that Emile Henry makes a line of ceramic French ovens called Flame Ceramic Cookware, made of local Burgundian clay and hardened by high temperatures to the point where these French ovens (they translate them as "stew pots") can withstand extreme temperature changes or thermal shock, meaning you can take them out of the freezer and put them

directly into a hot oven. The company spent over five years researching and developing the technology to create these qualities.

Emile Henry French ovens have their own immediately recognizable look, rounded, rustic, made in earthy colors like fig, black, deep olive, and red, with a distinctive shield on the lids, and are attractive enough to cook in then bring to the table to serve from. They are significantly lighter than enameled cast iron French ovens. What I love is that each one is made by hand and signed on the bottom with the initials of the person who made it. Emile Henry also makes mini cocottes.

Their French ovens can be used up to a temperature of 930° F (498° C), can be put on the barbecue or in the microwave, and are dishwasher safe. If you want to use them on an induction stovetop, you must purchase an induction disk to use under them.

Emile Henry Flame French ovens have a 10-year guarantee from date of purchase against breakage due to faulty manufacture.

Note: Like enameled cast iron French ovens, Emile Henry's ceramic French ovens should be gradually heated with something in them, from low to medium, as they have been designed for slow-cooking and simmering. Allow them to cool before washing.

FONTIGNAC

Fontignac French ovens are a terrific value, priced well below the top French brands yet performing up to my standards in every way. I first came across one when I was renting a holiday apartment

at a ski resort in France and used it there for making fondue as well as for stew. When I returned home I bought one, and now have a brand-new one I use just for making bread—see it in action by checking my recipe for Homemade Basil Garlic Bread (page 73).

Fontignac French ovens have been made in France since 1926 (it's written on the lid). Fontignac was originally Nomar, a small company making French ovens near Lyon before Staub bought them in 1988. Nomar used to make Paul Bocuse cocottes, which are a great vintage find as are some of the original Nomar French ovens. Fontignac is now part of the same group, Zwilling J.A. Henckels, which owns Staub.

Fontignac French ovens have well-sized handles made large enough for you to easily slip kitchen mitts into. The body of the oven is heavy and the self-basting lid fits well. And you can get them with stainless steel fleur-de-lis knobs.

Fontignac French ovens are safe up to 500° F (260° C) and are dishwasher safe. Their warranty is for 10 years.

Le Creuset

What is so special about the small village of Fresnoy-le-Grand in Picardy in the north of France? It is home to one of the largest manufacturers of French ovens, Le Creuset.

The company began in 1925 when a Belgian cast iron specialist, Armand Desaegner, and an enameling expert, Octave Aubecq, came together with the idea of pooling their talents to open a foundry to make enameled cast iron cookware.

It eventually also produced cast iron charcoal stoves, hot plates, and kitchen utensils until it decided to concentrate solely on making enameled cast iron cookware. In 1934, they introduced their famous bright orange flame colored cookware, still one of their signature colors.

As with the other French ovens, Le Creuset French ovens are one of a kind. They are made in a sand mold and crafted by hand. The enameling process covers everything, including the rims. The colors are vibrant, from Caribbean blue to sunny yellow, with limited edition colors popping up now and again. Interiors are sand colored.

Le Creuset French ovens are also produced in novelty shapes, including one in the shape of a flower, a pumpkin, a bell pepper, and an apple. They also make a line of mini cocottes, for which there are many recipes in this cookbook. The mini cocottes are made of stoneware and are not for use on the stovetop. They are meant for the oven and for presenting food, and can go straight from the freezer or refrigerator right into the oven then be placed on the table.

Le Creuset French ovens feel heavy, safe, and sturdy, although Le Creuset says on their website that their French ovens are "the lightest weight per quart of any premium cast iron cookware available."

They can be used on all heat sources, from open flame, outdoor grill, electric, gas, ceramic, halogen, induction stovetop, and oven. The phenolic knobs are oven safe to 390° F (198° C). The knob on the Signature series lid is safe in oven temperatures up to 480° F (249° C) and you can buy stainless steel knobs to replace both of these, which can be used at any temperature.

Based on anecdote as well as fact, it appears that Le Creuset has one of the best warranties. There is a lifetime limited warranty in the U.S., and if the French oven needs repair or needs to be replaced, you mail it to Le Creuset and they will either repair or replace it for you. Le Creuset customer service is well-known for being responsive and caring.

Le Creuset French ovens are dishwasher safe and Le Creuset cookware cleaner is available at most stores that sell Le Creuset.

MAUVIEL

The quintessential image of a restaurant in a French *auberge* or of a kitchen in a fabulous château is of lines of gleaming copper pots hanging from the ceiling or lining the walls.

In Normandy in northwestern France, coppersmiths have been making culinary copper pots since the 1300s in the village of Villedieu-les-Poêles. Visitors today can tour the beautifully preserved medieval town, its copper workshops, and the Museum of Copper Pots and Pans.

This is where Mauviel is located, in the "city of copper." The seventh-generation family-owned Mauviel has been manufacturing copper cookware there since 1830. They make stunningly beautiful French ovens, in round and oval sizes as well as copper or stainless steel mini cocottes. The Mauviel 1830 oval comes in 2.1 quart (1.9 l), 4.2 quart (3.9 l) and 7 quart (6.6 l) sizes and the Mauviel 1830 round French oven comes in 3.6 quart (3.4 l) and 5.5 quart (5.2 l) sizes.

The benefit of having a copper French oven is that copper acts almost the opposite of enameled cast iron French ovens that are brought up to heat slowly and cool down slowly. Copper, on the other hand, is quick and responsive. And while enameled cast iron French ovens are typically heavy to lift, copper is much lighter.

Mauviel's 1830 French ovens are top of the line and at the top of the price range. They are made 90 percent from thick professional-weight copper, are lined 10 percent with stainless steel, and have bronze handles.

They are oven safe to 500° F (260° C) and are broiler safe. On the stovetop, they work on electric, gas, and halogen, and although there is an induction disk for them, it is not recommended to use them on induction stovetops. It is also not recommended to put them in the dishwasher, but rather hand wash. Mauviel sells its Copperbrill copper cleaner at online stores.

There is a lifetime warranty for manufacturing defects, and Mauviel will repair or replace their French ovens under normal usage.

REVOL

In southeastern France in the small town of Saint-Uze in the Rhône-Alpes, a thriving ceramics industry developed due to the natural abundance of soft white clay called kaolin. Its white color is perfect for making china and porcelain. Ceramic objects have been found in this area since 4,500 BC, and in the seventeenth and eighteenth centuries workshops and small factories began producing pottery and cooking vessels there.

Today, it is one of the most important ceramic producing centers in France, and is home to Revol, which manufactures culinary porcelain and some of my favorite French ovens. When I cook with and bring to the table my snow-white Revol French oven, I can imagine and connect to the white kaolin it came from.

Revol, while known for its modern designs, dates back to 1789 when it was founded by the Revol family. Flash forward and you find that it is still owned and run by the eleventh generation of the family, while many of the workers in their factory are also in positions handed down from generation to generation.

Revol spent years researching for a way to produce high-performance culinary cooking vessels. They call the resulting process Revolution, because it achieves resistance to thermal shock, is totally nonporous, as well as being able to be used on all heat sources. Revol's Revolution French ovens are light to pick up, beautiful to look at with a totally different appearance than other French ovens, are a pleasure to cook in, and are made from a high-temperature–fired ceramic that withstands oven and broiler temperatures up to 572° F (299° C). They are also dishwasher safe.

Each one is unique and hand finished by one of approximately 200 people who work for Revol. While their iconic white ramekins and lion's head onion soup bowls have been made for over 100 years, their "crumple" cups and Revolution French ovens are their newest, most innovative products. They also make Revolution mini cocottes.

Revol has a 5-year warranty with proof of purchase and a photo of damage. You pay postage to return the piece to the factory in France, which will be refunded if the piece is found defective. Breakage due to defective manufacturing will result in replacement.

Note: Like enameled cast iron French ovens, Revol's ceramic Revolution French ovens should be gradually heated with something in them, from low to medium, as they have been designed for slow-cooking and simmering. Allow them to cool before washing.

STAUB

Staub's lineage is not as long as some of the others, but its popularity has skyrocketed with serious cooks and professional chefs.

It all began in Alsace in northern France in the early 1970s. Francis Staub's relatives had a dish store in Colmar, so he was in the frame of mind of thinking of ways to meet a need and being able to sell into that need. At that time, while there was a healthy demand for cast iron cooking pots, supply was not keeping up. So he thought about it and came up with a way to perfect cast iron cooking pots by putting a row of small spikes on the inside of the lid to draw down condensation to continually self-baste the food below. He opened a company in his name to design cast iron pots with these lids and outsourced the production.

All went well until the early 1980s when the microwave changed the way people cooked, from simmering on the back burner to quick and fast food cooking. The demand for cast iron pots dwindled. Despite that, he continued on, and in 1988 he acquired a company called Nomar, now known as Fontignac.

By 1995 he noticed business for enameled cast iron pots was picking up. His enameled cast iron French ovens became so in demand that in 2008 Monsieur Staub sold his company to the German group Zwilling J.A. Henckels. Staub today is still headquartered in Turckheim in Alsace and has three production facilities in France.

It is considered the top of the line by most professional and home chefs, immediately recognizable by its deep jewel-like glazes and its black matte interior finish. Staub's oval Coq au Vin French oven is known for its rooster "coq" knob perched on its lid—while fans also collect additional knobs that are available in the shape of either a fish or a pig. Staub metal handles can go in the oven to 500° F (260° C) and the ovens can be used on the stovetop on gas, electric, or induction. Each piece is unique, cast in a single-use sand mold, which is then destroyed, and is finished with two or three enamel coatings. And, of course, Staub makes mini cocottes.

Staub provides a lifetime limited warranty, with free repair or replacement if judged defective.

Note: Do not use Staub in the microwave. Before using it for the first time, Staub recommends that you lightly oil the black interior. While it is dishwasher safe, Staub recommends that you hand wash instead as dishwashers may, over time, affect the interior enamel.

HOW TO CHOOSE YOUR FRENCH OVEN

One of the first things to consider when purchasing a French oven is weight. If it will be difficult for you to lift an enameled cast iron French oven filled with food from the stove to the oven and back again then you might want to pick one of the lighter ovens made from ceramics or copper.

Although enameled cast iron French ovens are lighter now than they used to be, they are still sturdy and safe on the stove, not likely to be knocked over when you are deep-frying or have a stew bubbling away. I keep one on the back burner and value its weight for this reason.

Also consider the size of the handles. Some are smaller and some are larger so that you can fit oven mitts into them.

If you have an induction stovetop, check to see if your French oven can be used on it. Most of them can.

And now that they come in so many colors, it is possible to find white French ovens to go with a white kitchen, modern colors to go with a modern kitchen, and earthy colors to fit into a rustic look. Some of the French manufacturers are even dreaming up seasonal colors that fit a spring, summer, fall, or winter decor or menu. For the mini cocottes, there is a rainbow of colors and materials to choose from. I even have a set of pearlized white and black ones that I use for New Year's Eve.

HOW TO CARE FOR YOUR FRENCH OVEN

When you take your new French oven out of the box, remove all labels and stickers from it before using. Wash it, rinse, and dry. Normally, French ovens are easy to clean and require only a sponge and hot soapy water.

French ovens should be gently brought up to temperature and used on medium- to medium-high heat, rather than at a high stovetop heat that can cause food scorching. They are the ideal vessel for slow cooking at low to medium temperatures. If you are searing or browning, you can do it on medium to medium-high heat. Only use French ovens on high stovetop temperatures to boil water or to reduce sauces. Instead, for high temperature cooking, use sturdy skillets.

On induction stovetops, take care to lift the French oven on and off it rather than sliding it, so as not to scratch the surface. Increase the heat gently on an induction stovetop, for about 4 minutes,

until turning up to desired heat, and do not cook on the maximum setting or use the booster option. Remember, Mauviel's copper French ovens are not recommended to be used on induction stovetops.

For all French ovens, use wooden or heat-resistant utensils.

After cooking, let your French oven cool for 15 minutes before using soapy water and a soft sponge or plastic scouring pad to clean it.

Use nonabrasive products to clean the ovens and do not use steel wool, abrasive pads, or abrasive cleaning agents as they may dull the interior. If food has become burnt on, try simmering some water and a little white vinegar and baking soda for a while in the French oven and try to move the food off the bottom with a wooden spoon then let it soak in this mixture overnight. If that does not work, try again by adding 1/2 inch (1.25 cm) hydrogen peroxide and 2 teaspoons baking soda to your French oven, bring to a simmer, and cook for 8–10 minutes then scrub with a brush. Make sure you have your vent turned on as it will smell as you do this. You should be able to clean the French oven this way and not scratch or damage the interior.

For Staub French ovens that have black interiors, use a little vinegar and gentle detergent with hot water to clean. If it develops a white film from cooking, add a little baking soda to hot water and clean with a sponge.

USING THIS COOKBOOK

The recipes in this cookbook are French inspired ones I created for 5 quart (5 l) to 6 quart (5.7 l) French ovens, the mid-range size that I thought would be the most widely owned and useful. Although I use this size French oven for almost all my cooking, and can feed 4 to 6 people with it, you should consider buying as big of one as you can afford, especially if you have a family to feed. A 7- or 9-quart (6.6- to 8.5-l) size gives you added flexibility, allowing you not to worry how big your roast or chicken is. And a larger size typically has a wider bottom, meaning you can sear and brown more at a time and make larger breads and pizzas. The 7-quart (6.6 l) size or larger are also good holiday sizes, easily accommodating large roasts and are attractive enough to serve them at the table.

You can adjust my recipes to cook in a smaller-size French oven, or double them to work in a larger one. They are pretty flexible in this regard.

The recipes for mini cocottes will work in all mini cocottes, which are generally around 1 cup or 8 ounces (236 ml) in size.

Another tip about cooking with French ovens: when roasting meats or poultry or cooking a whole piece of fish, think more about the size that will fit into your French oven rather than the amount of pounds. I carry a small tape measure in my purse and pull it out to measure a leg of lamb or turkey I want to cook in my French oven. I provide weight measures for all my recipes, but encourage you, when you are roasting, to consider the size of the roast as well.

APPETIZERS IN

MINI COCOTTES

M y surprise and frustration at not being able to find more than one small cookbook in French about cooking in mini cocottes, and one small cookbook by one of the French oven manufacturers with some recipes for them, inspired me to devote two chapters in this cookbook to celebrate their versatility—this one for savory recipes and a later chapter for desserts.

You can make almost anything in a mini cocotte, from individual servings of lasagna to cheese fondue, baked eggs, or French onion soup topped with melted cheese. Or, you could fill them with smörgåsbord and set them out in a long line on the table for people to share. You can serve them in the living room in front of the fire or bring them to the table once family and guests are seated.

They come in all materials, including copper, stainless steel, stoneware, and enameled cast iron, and in a large variety of colors. In this chapter you will find my recipes for savory appetizers you can make and serve in mini cocottes for first courses, light lunches, or even for snacks.

VEGETABLE AND FETA CHEESE POT PIES

Petites Tourtes aux Légumes et à la Feta SERVES 6

Pot pies are one of my favorite comfort foods. This one is based on a French velouté sauce made with butter, flour, and vegetable stock to which you add mixed vegetables, marinated artichoke hearts, and crumbled feta then bake it with a golden puff pastry crust. It is a hearty appetizer before a light main course or can be a lunch dish served with a green salad.

SPECIAL EQUIPMENT 6 MINI COCOTTES; BAKING SHEET OR ROASTING PAN; PASTRY BRUSH

2 cups (480 ml) vegetable stock

20 fresh baby carrots (from a 16-ounce / 450-g bag), sliced in half vertically then both halves sliced into thirds

2 small red potatoes, peeled, cut into ½-inch (1.5-cm) slices, then diced

5 tablespoons (75 g) unsalted butter

2 medium shallots, minced

5 large cloves garlic, pressed or finely chopped

5 tablespoons (40 g) all-purpose flour

1 cup (240 ml) dry white wine, dry sherry, or white vermouth, plus more, if desired

Dash of cayenne

½ teaspoon salt

Freshly ground black pepper, to taste

1 tablespoon fresh tarragon leaves, finely chopped

1 cup (150 g) frozen baby peas

1 (12-ounce / 340-g) jar marinated artichoke hearts, drained and quartered

8 ounces (225 g) feta cheese

2 sheets frozen ready-to-bake puff pastry, thawed

1 large egg beaten with 1 teaspoon water for an egg wash

PREP

Preheat oven to 400° F (200° C), butter insides of cocottes, and place them on the baking sheet.

COOK

Heat vegetable stock in a medium saucepan to a boil. Add the carrots, bring back to a simmer, and cook for 5 minutes. Lift out with a slotted spoon and reserve.

Add the potatoes to the stock, bring back to a simmer, and cook for 5 minutes, or until tender. Lift out with a slotted spoon and reserve. Pour the vegetable stock into a bowl or measuring cup.

Wipe out the saucepan, melt the butter over low heat, then add the shallots and garlic and cook for 4 minutes. Shake in the flour and whisk while cooking for 1 minute. Slowly add the reserved vegetable stock and wine and whisk while cooking. Add the cayenne, salt, pepper, and tarragon and cook until sauce is thickened, about 2 minutes. Stir in the potatoes, carrots, and peas and taste. Add more wine if sauce needs to be thinned and salt and pepper, if desired.

Divide the artichoke hearts between the cocottes then ladle the vegetable mixture over the top. Crumble the feta cheese over the top of the vegetables.

Unfold the puff pastry on a lightly floured work surface. If cracks have developed, dip your finger in water then lightly press along the cracks to bring back together. Slice each sheet into quarters (you will have 2 leftover pieces). Place a piece of puff pastry over each mini cocotte, hanging it over the edge a bit, and press into the cocotte all the way around the edges. Brush each pastry with the egg wash.

Bake the pot pies for 15–20 minutes, until golden brown and puffed.

IDEAS AND SUGGESTIONS

You can make these ahead and keep them in the refrigerator until ready to bake.

To save time, buy a precooked rotisserie chicken and use the meat to make chicken pot pies, or use turkey and cranberries leftover from holidays.

CRUSTLESS SMOKED SALMON AND ZUCCHINI QUICHE

Quiche sans Pâte au Saumon Fumé et aux Courgettes SERVES 6

There was a pizzeria in Peymeinade, the village next to ours, on a busy main road that challenged diners to visit it. You risked your life trying to find a parking spot or even to navigate the traffic to cross over the street to it. Yet time and again we went back for a crazy pizza they made with zucchini, smoked salmon, wisps of red onion, and generous dollops of crème fraîche. Then they'd batter dip and fry zucchini flowers and strew them across the top. Their salty crispness against the soft pillows of crème fraîche and smoked salmon was an inspiration.

Inspired by that pizza, I created this quiche. I don't always have zucchini flowers, so with regret, I dropped that idea, but I did come up with a lovely appetizer you can make in mini cocottes that has the same luxurious taste.

Once these quiche come out of the oven, they will deflate a little. While you wait for them to cool to the touch, you could add a simple garnish to the center of a 1/2 teaspoon of sour cream and a frond of dill. There is sour cream in the recipe that will float up during baking to make a luscious warm cloud that surrounds the salmon and zucchini, putting a new spin on traditional quiche.

SPECIAL EQUIPMENT 6 MINI COCOTTES; BAKING SHEET OR ROASTING PAN; BOX GRATER

- 1 tablespoon extra virgin olive oil, plus extra to coat cocottes
- 2 medium zucchini
- 1/2 lemon, squeezed
- 4 ounces (110 g) smoked salmon, sliced into 1/2-inch (1.5-cm) pieces, divided
- 9 heaping tablespoons (180 g) sour cream, divided
- 4 large eggs
- 1 1/2 cups (360 ml) half-and-half
- 1/8 teaspoon freshly grated nutmeg
- 1/2 teaspoon salt
- 2 cracks freshly ground pepper
- 2 tablespoons (15 g) all-purpose flour

PREP

Preheat oven to 350° F (180° C), grease mini cocottes with oil, and place them on the baking sheet.

Grate zucchini, unpeeled, on large holes of a box grater. You should have about (2 cups / 350 g). Squeeze dry in paper towels to eliminate excess water.

COOK

Toss zucchini with the lemon juice and divide in half. Evenly layer the bottoms of the cocottes with half of the zucchini, without compacting it too much.

Using half of the salmon, arrange a layer over the top of the zucchini in each cocotte. Spoon 1 heaping tablespoon sour cream over the top of the salmon in each cocotte. Repeat a layer of zucchini over the sour cream then arrange the remaining salmon pieces over the zucchini. Spoon 1/2 tablespoon sour cream over the salmon pieces.

In a bowl, beat the eggs with a fork or a whisk. Pour in oil, half-and-half, nutmeg, salt, and pepper and whisk to combine. Sift in the flour and whisk until there are no lumps. Divide the egg mixture over the top of each cocotte, filling all the way to the top. Place on the baking sheet and bake for 27 minutes, or until golden and puffed. Serve as soon as the cocottes are cool enough to touch.

IDEAS AND SUGGESTIONS

For garnishes, try a small salad of delicate greens heaped on top of each, or a spoonful of red caviar.

FONDUE MAC 'N' CHEESE

Macaronis au Fromage, comme une Fondue SERVES 6

I used to make fondue or mac 'n' cheese for comfort food when it was freezing outside and it had snowed for days and days. Then I had dinner at a friend's house and she mixed the two. Brilliant. So now I nudge the flavorings of this mac 'n' cheese into a fondue landscape by using the traditional cheeses used to make fondue in the heart of the French Alps, add a splash of Kirsch to seal the deal, and serve it bubbling and golden in mini cocottes.

SPECIAL EQUIPMENT 6 MINI COCOTTES; BAKING SHEET

3 cups (450 g) small elbow macaroni

2 tablespoons (30 ml) extra virgin olive oil

1 large clove garlic, pressed or minced

¼ teaspoon Dijon mustard

1 teaspoon freshly grated nutmeg

4 tablespoons (60 g) unsalted butter, divided

3 tablespoons (25 g) all-purpose flour

1½ cups (360 ml) half-and-half

1 cup (240 ml) dry white wine

2 tablespoons (30 ml), or more to taste, Kirsch, cherry brandy, or cognac

1 cup (100 g) coarsely grated Gruyère cheese

1 cup (100 g) coarsely grated Emmenthal cheese

1 cup (100 g) coarsely grated Comté cheese

¾ cup (60 g) panko crumbs

1 teaspoon salt

Paprika

PREP

Preheat oven to 400° F (200° C), generously butter the cocottes, and place them on the baking sheet.

COOK

Cook macaroni in well-salted water according to package instructions, about 10 minutes. Drain.

In a saucepan, heat the olive oil over medium heat. Add the garlic and cook for 1 minute. Add mustard, nutmeg, and 2 tablespoons (30 g) butter, melting as you stir. Whisk in flour and cook for 2 minutes. Pour in the half-and-half, wine, and Kirsch and whisk over medium heat until it thickens. Toss in the cheeses and energetically whisk until well blended and smooth. Taste for seasoning and adjust.

Scoop the macaroni into the pot and stir well to completely coat with the cheese sauce.

Melt remaining butter in another saucepan. Toss the panko crumbs in the butter, sprinkle with salt, and toss again to coat.

Spoon the macaroni into the cocottes and top with the panko crumbs. Sprinkle each with a little paprika and place the cocottes in the oven to bake for 13–15 minutes, or until they are golden and bubbling.

IDEAS AND SUGGESTIONS

You can also add a small handful of minced herbs or crushed green peppercorns, or switch out one of the cheeses for grated mozzarella to make it gooey delicious.

WARM SCALLOP MOUSSE WITH ROASTED CHERRY TOMATOES

Mousse Tiède de Coquilles Saint-Jacques et Tomates Cerises Rôties SERVES 6

Equally good made with cod, salmon, lobster, or crab, this silky smooth scallop mousse is a French seafood classic. Present it in its mini cocotte placed on a folded white napkin on each plate for a luxurious dinner party or to set the stage for a romantic evening. The slight roasted sweetness of the cherry tomatoes nicely offsets the richness of the mousse.

SPECIAL EQUIPMENT 6 MINI COCOTTES; PARCHMENT PAPER OR ALUMINUM FOIL; ROASTING PAN; FOOD PROCESSOR; BAKING SHEET

1 pound (450 g) sea scallops, refrigerated for 1 hour

1 large egg, chilled

1 large egg white, chilled

1 teaspoon kosher or sea salt, plus more for garnish

Freshly ground white pepper

Pinch of cayenne pepper

¼ teaspoon freshly grated nutmeg

1 cup (240 g) heavy cream, refrigerated 1 hour

6 cherry tomatoes

3 tablespoons (45 ml) extra virgin olive oil, plus more for coating tomatoes, divided

6 fresh basil leaves

PREP

Preheat oven to 325° F (160° C). Generously butter the mini cocottes and place them in the refrigerator until ready to fill. With scissors, cut 6 rounds of parchment paper or aluminum foil that will fit over each cocotte and butter one side of them.

Boil enough water to pour into the roasting pan, halfway up the cocottes, which will allow the little mousses to cook more gently.

COOK

Put the scallops into the food processor and blend until very smooth, for about 10 seconds. Add the egg, egg white, salt, pepper, cayenne, nutmeg, and cream and process 5 seconds. Scrape down and process 3 seconds.

Place the cocottes in the roasting pan. Spoon the scallop mixture into the cocottes and top with the buttered parchment paper rounds, which will help protect them from browning on the top. Pour the boiling water around cocottes in the roasting pan and place in the oven to cook for 20 minutes, until the mousse is set and a tester comes out clean. Take out of the oven, and when cool enough to touch, place on serving plates until the cherry tomatoes are ready.

Meanwhile, turn up the oven to 400° F (200° C). Coat the cherry tomatoes in oil, place on a baking sheet, sprinkle with salt, and roast in the oven for 15 minutes.

Finely chop the basil like confetti. Drop it into a bowl, pour in 3 tablespoons (45 ml) olive oil and sea salt and whisk.

Place 1 roasted cherry tomato on the top of each mousse and drizzle the basil in oil across the top horizontally before serving.

IDEAS AND SUGGESTIONS

You can make these the day before and reheat them.

SUMMER GARDEN CRUDITÉS WITH LYONNAISE HERB DIP

Crudités d'un Jardin d'Été, Sauce Lyonnaise aux Herbes SERVES 6

I like to set these out in a part of the house or outside where we can watch the sun go down with a glass of wine. Everyone has their own mini cocotte of vegetables and bowl of dip to drag them through. It's a lazy end-of-the-week kind of starter, light enough not to spoil your meal later, with just enough to keep hunger at bay.

If you can find new carrots with their stems and leaves on, or rainbow radishes with their stems and leaves on, or fresh fragrant herbs to tuck in, these add a beautiful element to the arrangements. Use more or less of any of the following, or whatever vegetables you have from your garden or farmers market.

SPECIAL EQUIPMENT 6 MINI COCOTTES; FOOD PROCESSOR OR BLENDER; 6 SMALL BOWLS

Lyonnaise Herb Dip

3 cups (27 ounces / 760 g) whole-milk ricotta cheese

6 ounces (170 g) soft goat cheese, room temperature

5 tablespoons (75 ml) extra virgin olive oil, plus more for drizzling

4 teaspoons (20 ml) red or white wine vinegar

3 large cloves garlic

2 medium shallots

2 tablespoons tarragon

3 tablespoons chives

Salt and coarsely ground black pepper, to taste

Cocottes

6 small carrots, sliced into 5-inch (12.5-cm) pieces

24 green or yellow string beans, trimmed

2 orange or red bell peppers, each sliced into 6 pieces

6 large radishes, sliced or carved into flowers

1 English cucumber, peeled and sliced into 4-inch (10-cm) pieces

2 large endive

1 small radicchio

6 sprigs fresh curly parsley

PREP

Slice bottoms off endive and radicchio and separate leaves.

COOK

Lyonnaise Herb Dip

Place everything into a food processor or blender and process until smooth. Use a little milk to thin out, if desired. Scoop into 6 small bowls and drizzle with olive oil.

Cocottes

Arrange the vegetables in the cocottes. Tuck a sprig of parsley into each and serve with the dip.

IDEAS AND SUGGESTIONS

Other vegetables to consider: fennel strips, broccoli florets, green or white asparagus spears, green or white cauliflower florets, strips of zucchini, whole pea pods, or Daikon radish.

MARINATED GOAT CHEESE WITH ROASTED GARLIC

Fromage de Chèvre mariné à l'Ail rôti SERVES 6

Easily served as an appetizer or as the cheese course after the main meal, these small cocottes of marinated goat cheese are served with toasts and little spreading knives. For this recipe, you slice off pieces from a large log of goat cheese, but if you can find them, feel free to substitute whole small goat cheese rounds with rinds.

Too often I come across goat cheese drizzled with balsamic or honey or sprinkled with cranberries. I prefer for this dish to concentrate on buying the best quality goat cheese, the best quality olive oil, and pairing them with some roasted garlic, fresh cherry tomatoes, and great bread. Simple and delicious.

SPECIAL EQUIPMENT ALUMINUM FOIL; BAKING SHEET; 6 MINI COCOTTES

2 fresh thyme sprigs

6 fresh basil leaves

6 cherry tomatoes

18 large cloves garlic

¾ cup (180 ml) best quality extra virgin olive oil, plus 3 tablespoons (45 ml), divided

3 teaspoons fine table salt, divided

2 tablespoons pink peppercorns, crushed

12 ounces (340 g) soft goat cheese, sliced into 6 even rounds

Flaky sea salt (like Maldon) for garnish

Baguette or hearty flavorful farmhouse bread thickly sliced and toasted

PREP

Preheat oven to 375° F (190° C) and place a piece of aluminum foil on the baking sheet.

With kitchen scissors, snip off tiny florets of thyme leaves. Discard the stalks. Divide leaves into 2 piles. Stack basil leaves, roll tightly, and then thinly slice into fine ribbons.

Finely slice cherry tomatoes then slice into small dice, reserving a few slices for garnish.

COOK

Place the whole cloves of garlic in a bowl, pour in 3 tablespoons (45 ml) oil, sprinkle in 2 teaspoons salt, and toss well to combine. Heap the garlic onto the center of the foil, pull the foil up and around the garlic to seal the package, and bake for 40–50 minutes, until soft. Remove from the oven, open the packet, and allow garlic to cool to room temperature.

In a bowl, whisk together the remaining oil, remaining salt, crushed pink peppercorns, and 1 pile of thyme leaves. Pour 1 tablespoon of this oil mixture into the bottom of each cocotte. Place a goat cheese round on top. Drizzle a little of the oil mixture over each goat cheese round.

Evenly distribute the basil ribbons, then the tomatoes, then the remaining pile of thyme florets into each cocotte. Place 3 roasted garlic cloves in each cocotte then sprinkle each cocotte with a little flaky sea salt. Garnish with a little of the sliced cherry tomatoes and some basil.

Serve with little spreading knives and toasted slices of baguette.

IDEAS AND SUGGESTIONS

Run the mini cocottes under the broiler briefly to slightly warm and melt the cheese. Small fresh burrata (mozzarella) balls can be added.

SHRIMP COCKTAIL WITH SPICY DIPPING SAUCE

Cocktail de Crevettes avec une Sauce épicée SERVES 6

One day I discovered that if I dropped a whole sliced lemon, including the peel, into the food processor while making a rémoulade sauce, it resulted in a spicy lemony dip I liked better than any I had before.

Rémoulade is a French sauce or dip typically made with mayonnaise, finely chopped sour gherkins, capers, mustard, shallots, fresh herbs, and sometimes finely chopped anchovies. Adding the lemon and changing the ingredients a little, then chilling it, makes a just about perfect dip for shrimp cocktail.

SPECIAL EQUIPMENT FOOD PROCESSOR; STAND MIXER; 6 MINI COCOTTES

2 organic lemons

3 teaspoons Dijon mustard

¼ cup (60 g) tomato ketchup

1 tablespoon paprika

⅛ teaspoon cayenne or hot pepper sauce

½ teaspoon salt or 4 canned anchovies, finely chopped

4 teaspoons sugar

1 stalk celery with leaves, sliced into 2-inch (5-cm) pieces and coarsely chop leaves for garnish

1 large clove garlic

⅛ cup (30 g) horseradish

2 large egg yolks

½ cup (120 ml) olive or vegetable oil

2 tablespoons capers, coarsely chopped

30 medium shrimp, boiled, drained, and peeled

6 leaves Boston or soft lettuce

PREP

Leave peel on lemons. Slice 1 lemon into 3 slices then slice each in half. Slice the other lemon into 6 wedges for garnish.

COOK

Toss the lemon slices into the food processor and process for 12 seconds. Add the mustard, ketchup, paprika, cayenne, salt, sugar, celery, garlic, and horseradish and process until smooth.

In the stand mixer bowl, beat the yolks until they start to thicken. Drizzle in the oil while beating until you have a mayonnaise consistency. Add the lemon mixture from the food processor and capers and mix well to combine. Refrigerate this dip and the cooked shrimp for 2 hours.

To serve, place 1 lettuce leaf into each cocotte, spoon the dip onto the leaves and arrange 5 shrimp, tail side up, around the edges of each cocotte. Sprinkle the chopped celery leaves on for garnish, add 1 lemon wedge to each, and serve.

IDEAS AND SUGGESTIONS

Add finely minced sour gherkins or garnish with a tiny sprinkle of Old Bay Seasoning.

MINI ANTIPASTO

Petit Antipasto SERVES 6

When I make antipasto for a casual gathering, I simply tear off a large piece of parchment paper or brown kitchen paper and lay it on the table, wrap prosciutto around bread sticks and pile them in the center, working outwards with large chunks of Parmigiano-Reggiano, sliced figs, and little bowls of marinated morsels. When I am setting a more formal table, I tuck everything into mini cocottes, like this.

SPECIAL EQUIPMENT 6 MINI COCOTTES

1 (6-ounce / 170-g) jar marinated artichokes, sliced into 12 even pieces

1 (7-ounce / 198-g) jar marinated sun-dried tomatoes

12 oil-cured black olives

12 slices prosciutto, rolled

12 slices salami, rolled

8 ounces (225 g) blue cheese, sliced into 6 equal pieces

8 ounces (225 g) Parmigiano-Reggiano cheese, sliced into 6 equal pieces

6 small bunches of seedless grapes

6 bread sticks

6 sprigs fresh thyme

1 bottle best quality aged balsamic vinegar

Slab of unsalted butter with a sprinkle of fleur de sel flakes over the top

Bowl or chopping board with baguette sliced on the diagonal

COOK

Place 2 artichoke pieces on the bottom of each cocotte. Evenly divide tomatoes into each cocotte. Add 2 olives then arrange 2 rolls of prosciutto and 2 rolls of salami into each cocotte, standing them up. Next, stand up wedges of blue cheese and Parmigiano-Reggiano.

Snuggle in the grapes. Slip 1 breadstick into each cocotte so that it stands tall on one side. Finally, slip in 1 sprig of thyme in each cocotte and serve.

Place the bottle of vinegar, butter, and slices of baguette on the table.

IDEAS AND SUGGESTIONS

Alternative ingredients could include mini mozzarella balls with a drizzle of olive oil at the bottom or fresh figs and apricots sliced into small chunks.

WARM MUSHROOM CUSTARDS WITH GARLIC BREAD

Petits Flans tièdes aux Champignons et Pain à l'Ail SERVES 6

During mushroom season in France, weekends were often spent in the hills foraging for mushrooms. We would go with friends because there were so many rules for picking, and so many varieties that were poisonous that we felt better letting them guide us. Still, we'd carry our harvest into a local pharmacy where trained experts would check the mushrooms for us.

The first meal I would make would be to sauté the mushrooms in a large skillet with oil, garlic, and parsley then very gently stir in beaten eggs to just pull them together. This simple meal gave so much pleasure it was one of the reasons we would spend all day harvesting. I would also plan a dinner the next day for friends to share our stash and this was the appetizer I came up with.

Shades of brown, bubbly, and silky smooth inside, I would serve these intriguing mushroom custards warm, each with a toasted soldier of garlic bread or on a large dinner plate as a side to grilled steak or lamb.

SPECIAL EQUIPMENT 6 MINI COCOTTES; BAKING PAN; FOOD PROCESSOR; PASTRY BRUSH; BAKING SHEET

Mushroom Custards

4 tablespoons (60 g) unsalted butter, softened, plus more to coat cocottes

8 ounces (225 g) white button mushrooms

3 cups (720 ml) half-and-half

2 large cloves garlic, sliced

½ teaspoon sweet paprika

Dash of cayenne

1 teaspoon dried thyme

2 chicken or vegetable bouillon cubes, coarsely chopped

6 large eggs, room temperature

Garlic Bread

2 tablespoon extra virgin olive oil

1 large clove garlic, pressed or minced

Salt, to taste

2 slices thick white sandwich bread

2 tablespoons minced flat-leaf parsley

3 sprigs curly parsley

PREP

Preheat oven to 300° F (150° C), butter mini cocottes, and place in baking pan. Boil enough water to reach halfway up cocottes in the baking pan.

Pull stems off mushrooms and coarsely chop. Thinly slice enough mushrooms into the cocottes to reach barely halfway to the top. Mince any remaining mushrooms and reserve.

COOK

Mushroom Custards

Heat half-and-half in a saucepan with the garlic, chopped mushroom stems, paprika, cayenne, and thyme. Stir in the bouillon. Let the mixture barely simmer for 8 minutes, process in the food processor, then return to the saucepan. Take the saucepan off the heat.

Whisk the eggs together then pour into the saucepan and whisk to combine. Pour this mixture into each cocotte then pour the boiling water into the baking pan to reach halfway up the sides of the cocottes. Put the pan in the oven to bake for 35 minutes. The custards are done when a knife comes out clean.

Garlic Bread

While the custards are cooking, mix oil with the garlic. Sprinkle in a little salt. Slice crusts from the bread. Cut each slice of bread vertically into 3 pieces. With the pastry brush, generously brush each slice with the oil and garlic mixture and place on the baking sheet. Place in the oven with the cocottes to bake until lightly golden. Remove and sprinkle the top thirds with minced parsley.

Serve the cocottes warm and balance 1 garlic bread on each.

IDEAS AND SUGGESTIONS

Add in some cremini and shiitake mushrooms.

SOUPS

The soups I make are generally a thicker and heartier variety, dense and full of texture. If I make a smooth one, I add in an unexpected flavor to make it more interesting. I love making soups and creating new ones with what I find at the market. I almost always make them in a French oven because it is big enough to cook a large batch and have leftovers to share with family and friends.

Soups are doubly delicious when beautifully served, so I often take the French oven right to the table along with a gorgeous heirloom ladle. A basket of warm biscuits to the side or small toasts or croutons for crunch, and I have the makings of a satisfying one-pot meal.

GORGEOUS CHILLED BEET SOUP WITH BEET GREENS SALAD

Délicieuse Soupe Glacée de Betteraves et Salade de Fanes de Betteraves SERVES 8

One hot summer night in Paris, I was served a chilled fuchsia-colored soup at a friend's apartment. It was one of those once in a lifetime experiences—high ceilings, a view of the Eiffel Tower sparkling in the distant darkness from the living room windows, and a long formal table set in the dining room for us to enjoy an elegant dinner with her family and friends.

The highlight of the meal was this refreshing chilled soup, brought to the table in delicate porcelain bowls shaped like lettuce leaves. On my way out, I asked what the ingredients were. "Just beets and lait fermenté!" Lait fermenté is fermented milk, tasting very much like our buttermilk. I began making it at home in a blender, and now whiz up a more rustic version in minutes in a food processor, topping each bowl with a raw chopped salad of beet greens and beets.

SPECIAL EQUIPMENT PARCHMENT PAPER OR WAX PAPER; BOX GRATER; 5-QUART (5-L) OR LARGER FRENCH OVEN; FOOD PROCESSOR

- 8 beets, with good looking leaves
- 2 tablespoons fresh lemon juice
- 2 quarts (2 l) buttermilk
- 2 tablespoons (25 g) sugar
- 1 teaspoon kosher or sea salt, plus ¼ teaspoon, divided
- 2 cracks freshly ground pepper
- 2 tablespoons (30 ml) extra virgin olive oil
- 1 tablespoon (15 ml) white or wine vinegar

PREP

Wash, trim, and peel the beets, wearing rubber gloves if you wish to keep your hands from turning red.

Place a piece of parchment paper or wax paper on your cutting board to protect it from the beet juice then coarsely shred 2 of the beets on a box grater and reserve for garnish. Slice remaining beets into large pieces.

Pull the leaves off the beet stems and discard stems. Finely chiffonade the beet greens. Keep a tightly packed ½ cup (30 g) for salad garnish and use the remaining greens for another purpose.

COOK

Place the sliced beets in the French oven with enough water to cover, pour in the lemon juice, and bring to a boil. Reduce to a simmer and cook the beets until they are tender. Depending on their size, it could take 40–60 minutes. Drain in a colander.

When the beets are cool enough to touch, put them in the food processor, in batches, with the buttermilk, sugar, 1 teaspoon salt, and pepper and process until very smooth, pouring the purée back into the French oven. Taste and season with more salt and pepper, if desired. Cover with the lid and refrigerate until well chilled.

When you are ready to serve the soup, prepare the beet greens salad. In a bowl, whisk together the oil, remaining salt, and vinegar. Toss in the grated beets and reserved beet greens. Mix well to coat.

Ladle soup into bowls. Heap the salad in the center of each bowl and serve.

IDEAS AND SUGGESTIONS

Make beet greens chips by baking them in the oven, massaged with a little olive oil and sprinkled with salt. Bake at 375° F (190° C) until crispy.

WHITE SOUP WITH POMEGRANATE SEEDS AND PISTACHIOS

Soupe Blanche, Graines de Grenade et Pistaches SERVES 6

Once I heard about potage à la reine, *I had to learn more. A seventeenth-century soup that was made in France with almond milk, ground almonds, and chicken? Creamy, yet not using cream? Was it on French menus today?*

I also read that it was a soup taught by Fannie Farmer at her cooking classes in Boston in the late nineteenth century, which gained fame due to being mentioned in Jane Austen's Pride and Prejudice *as "white soup."*

Piecing together the information I could gather, I came up with this recipe. I know for a fact that it was served at aristocratic tables in seventeenth-century France with a garnish of pomegranate seeds and pistachios, and that it was made with almond milk, which was popular then because it did not spoil like cow's milk.

What I came up with is a gentle, almost healing soup. It is gluten free and creamless, thickened only by ground chicken and almonds. It has a very unusual texture that I am totally enamored with.

SPECIAL EQUIPMENT 5-QUART (5-L) OR LARGER FRENCH OVEN; FOOD PROCESSOR

- 6 bone-in chicken thighs
- 1 pomegranate or store-bought fresh pomegranate seeds
- Shelled pistachios
- 1 cup (190 g) uncooked medium-grain white rice
- 5 cups (1.2 l) water
- 2 chicken bouillon cubes
- 4 ounces (110 g) whole almonds
- 1½ teaspoons kosher or sea salt
- 1 cup (240 ml) unsweetened almond milk

PREP

Remove skin from the chicken thighs and discard. Slice halfway along the bone to enable the chicken to cook better.

Slice pomegranate in half and, with a fork, scoop out the seeds into a bowl of water. This technique allows the white bits to float up to the top so that you can scoop them away and it does not affect the color of the seeds left below. Drain and reserve the seeds for garnish.

Slice the pistachios with the intention of having small chunks or slices of green to garnish the top of each soup bowl.

COOK

Place the chicken, rice, water, and bouillon cubes into the French oven. Bring to a boil over medium heat, reduce to a simmer, and cook 15–20 minutes, or until chicken is cooked through and the rice is tender.

Lift out the chicken to drain in a colander. When it is cool to touch, slice the meat off the bones of 4 of the thighs, discard the bones, and toss the chicken meat into the food processor. Process for 10 seconds.

For the remaining chicken thighs, shred the meat off the bones and then coarsely chop. Reserve.

Ladle half the contents from the French oven into the food processor with the already processed chicken, add the almonds, and process for 20 seconds, until very smooth. Pour everything back into the French oven.

Add the salt, reserved chicken, and almond milk. Stir to blend, and taste for seasoning. If desired, add more salt or a bit more almond milk or water if it is too thick. It should be the consistency of a thin porridge. Make sure it is hot before you serve it.

Ladle the soup into each bowl. Scatter pomegranate seeds and pistachios over the top and serve.

IDEAS AND SUGGESTIONS

If you have any pomegranate seeds leftover, store in plastic bags in the refrigerator for up to 2 months. They're great whisked into salad dressings or added when you cook rice.

ARTICHOKE PARMESAN SOUP

Soupe à l'Artichaut et au Parmesan SERVES 8

When I was a newlywed there was a warm dip everyone made for parties, called artichoke dip. It was a combination of artichokes, mayonnaise, and grated Parmesan cheese. This recipe developed from my desire to recreate that seductive flavor in a soup. It is much healthier than the dip and it satisfies my yearning to capture that memory and bring it to life in a different guise. Once you make it, you will want to make it again and again.

SPECIAL EQUIPMENT FOOD PROCESSOR; 5-QUART (5-L) FRENCH OVEN; STAND MIXER

4 (14-ounce / 400-g) cans artichoke hearts, drained

2 tablespoons (30 ml) extra virgin olive oil, plus 1/4 cup (60 ml), divided

4 cups (1 l) chicken or vegetable stock

1 (15.5 ounce / 440-g) can cannellini beans

1 cup (100 g) grated Parmesan cheese

1 organic lemon, zested and juiced

1/2 teaspoon salt

2 egg yolks, room temperature

1/2 teaspoon Dijon mustard

1 (12-ounce / 340-g) bottle marinated artichoke hearts

COOK

Place half of the drained artichokes and 1 tablespoon (15 ml) olive oil in the food processor and process for a 1 1/2 minutes, scraping down halfway. Scoop into French oven.

Repeat this process with the rest of the drained artichokes and 1 tablespoon (15 ml) olive oil. Scoop into French oven then pour in the stock.

Process the beans in the food processor until smooth, scoop into French oven, and stir to combine. Add the cheese, 1 tablespoon (15 ml) lemon juice, and salt and whisk to combine. Heat over medium until it comes to a boil then turn down to a simmer.

Meanwhile, beat the egg yolks and mustard using the stand mixer for 2 minutes. Very slowly add in the remaining oil while continuously beating until it turns into a mayonnaise consistency. When you turn down the soup to a simmer, whisk this into the soup and continue to cook for 3 minutes, whisking frequently.

Squeeze dry the marinated artichoke hearts in paper towels then coarsely chop. Toss together with 1 tablespoon (15 ml) lemon juice and the lemon zest.

Make sure to bring the soup back to a boil before serving so that the cheese completely melts. Ladle hot soup into bowls and garnish the centers with a heap of the chopped marinated artichokes.

IDEAS AND SUGGESTIONS

Another garnish idea is to shave long strips of Parmigiano-Reggiano cheese with a vegetable peeler and heap them in the center of each bowl.

FRENCH CARROT RICE SOUP WITH HOMEMADE CROUTONS

Soupe à la Carotte et au Riz à la Française, Croûtons Maison SERVES 6 TO 8

The classic French soup, potage Crécy, was named for the celebrated carrots grown in Crécy, France. Traditionally, it is a silky smooth puréed soup served in delicate bowls. My version, instead, is rustic and quite thick, a meal in itself with the added appeal of delicious crunchy homemade croutons.

SPECIAL EQUIPMENT 5-QUART (5-L) OR LARGER FRENCH OVEN; FOOD PROCESSOR

4 slices good sandwich bread

8 tablespoons (120 g) unsalted butter

1½ pounds (700 g) carrots, sliced into ¼-inch (½-cm) pieces

2 medium white onions, finely chopped

2 whole cloves

¼ teaspoon ground cloves

⅔ cups (130 g) uncooked rice (I use brown basmati, but any rice will do)

4 cups (1 l) chicken broth

1 tablespoon fresh thyme leaves, divided

1 teaspoon kosher or sea salt, plus more to sprinkle croutons

¼ teaspoon pepper

1 teaspoon sugar

1 medium carrot, small dice

2 tablespoons (30 ml) extra virgin olive oil

½ cup (120 g) half-and-half

PREP

Slice the crusts off the bread and slice into crouton cubes: either large, small, or tiny.

COOK

In the French oven, melt the butter over medium heat. Add the sliced carrots, onions, whole cloves, ground cloves, rice, broth, half of the thyme, salt, pepper, and sugar. Put the lid on and simmer for 30 minutes, until the carrots are soft.

In a small saucepan, heat enough water to cover the diced carrot and cook until soft, about 15 minutes. Drain and reserve.

Heat oil in a skillet, sprinkle with some salt, toss in the croutons, and cook on medium heat until golden brown. Reserve on paper towels.

Remove the cloves from the soup and discard. Purée the soup in small batches in the food processor for about 10 seconds per batch, until not totally smooth. You want to still have small flecks of carrots and some rice texture in the soup. Return each batch to the pot. Whisk in the half-and-half and taste for seasoning, adding more salt and pepper, if desired.

Ladle soup into bowls and garnish each with the diced carrots, remaining thyme leaves, and croutons.

IDEAS AND SUGGESTIONS

Add ½ tablespoon grated ginger and change the sugar to brown sugar for a variation on the theme.

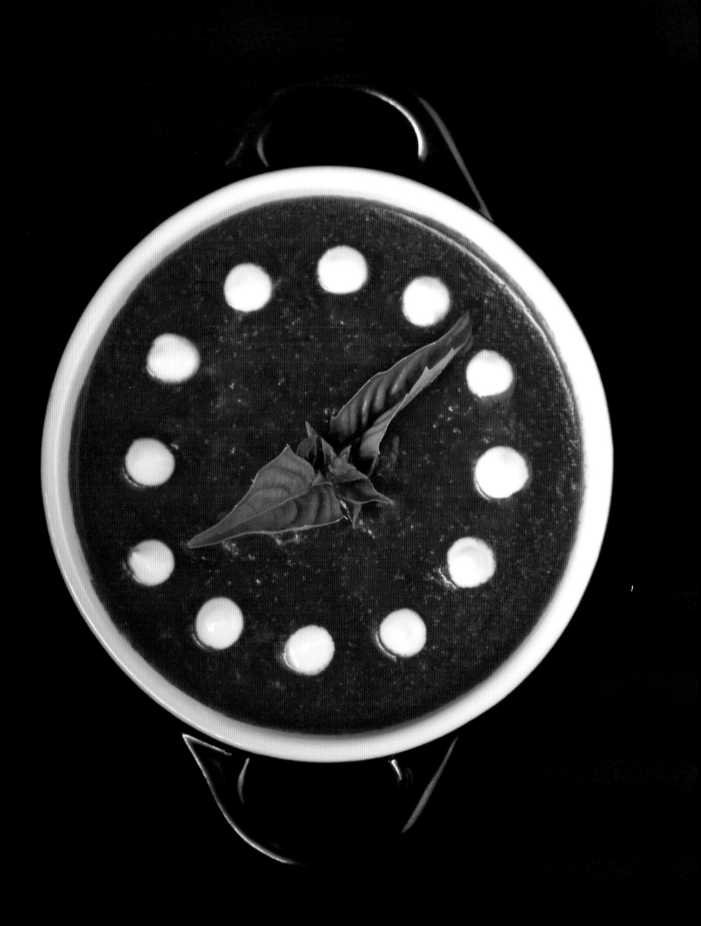

CREAM OF RED CABBAGE, TOMATO, AND BEEF MARROW BONE SOUP

Crème de Chou Rouge, Tomate et Os à Moëlle de Boeuf SERVES 6

One of the benefits of cooking soup in a French oven is that you have lots of room. This soup is a version of one my grandmother used to make, mine adding in tomato and big beef marrow bones that just fit in the French oven. They add a wonderful beefy flavor and nutrients to the soup.

I cook it in my French oven then serve it in mini cocottes with dollops of sour cream, which goes well with the red cabbage and tomatoes.

SPECIAL EQUIPMENT 5-QUART (5-L) FRENCH OVEN; FOOD PROCESSOR OR BLENDER

- 2 beef marrow bones that will fit in your French oven, washed and patted dry
- 6 cups (1.5 l) beef stock
- 2 medium carrots, thickly sliced
- 1 large white onion, thickly sliced
- 2 cups (180 g) chopped red cabbage
- 2 pounds (900 g) tomatoes, thickly sliced, saving juice and seeds
- 4 tablespoons (50 g) sugar
- 1 cup (240 g) sour cream, plus more for garnish, if desired
- ¼ cup (30 g) all-purpose flour
- Salt and pepper, to taste

COOK

To the French oven, add the bones, stock, carrots, onion, and cabbage. Bring to a boil over medium heat, reduce to a simmer, and cook for 30 minutes.

Remove the bones from the soup. Dig the marrow out of the bones and put back into the soup. Discard the bones.

Add the tomatoes, with juice and seeds, and sugar. Purée the soup in batches in a food processor or blender (it doesn't need to be silky smooth) and return to the pot.

Whisk 1 cup sour cream with the flour then whisk into the soup. Bring soup just to a boil then turn down to a simmer, and whisk until slightly thickened, about 5 minutes. Add salt and pepper, whisking to combine.

Ladle the soup into bowls and serve, with a dollop of sour cream, if desired.

RADISH LEAF, POTATO, AND LEEKS SOUP WITH SHREDDED RADISH SALAD

Soupe de Fanes de Radis, Pommes de Terre et Poireaux, Salade de Radis râpés

SERVES 4

A variation on a French country soup made with potatoes and leeks, my radish leaf soup adds in the peppery, slightly bitter flavor of radish leaves. It's wonderfully satisfying served hot or cold and has a final drizzle of extra virgin olive oil with a garnish of raw grated radishes and golden croutons.

Look for the freshest radishes you can find, and if possible, use ones out of your garden. Pick over the leaves for those in the best condition, tossing the rest.

SPECIAL EQUIPMENT BOX GRATER, 5-QUART (5-L) OR LARGER FRENCH OVEN, BLENDER OR FOOD PROCESSOR

2 bunches radishes

3 cups (90 g) tightly packed radish leaves

3 tablespoons (45 g) unsalted butter

4 medium red potatoes, peeled and thinly sliced into 1/8-inch (3-mm) thick slices

2 medium leeks, sliced into 1/4-inch (.5-cm) thick slices

1 large clove garlic, thinly sliced

1/2 teaspoon Dijon mustard

1 1/2 cups (360 ml) water, divided

1 chicken bouillon cube

1 1/2 cups (360 ml) whole milk

2 egg yolks

1/2 cup (120 g) sour cream, plus 6 tablespoons (90 g)

Kosher or sea salt and plenty of coarsely ground black pepper, to taste

4 slices sourdough bread

2 tablespoons (30 ml) extra virgin olive oil

1 teaspoon kosher or sea salt

Olive oil

PREP

Wash the radishes and their leaves. Pat dry. Slice the radish leaves off the stems and discard stems. Coarsely chop the leaves. Shred the radishes on a box grater and reserve.

COOK

In the French oven, melt the butter then add the potatoes, leeks, radish leaves, garlic, mustard, and 1 cup (240 ml) water. Crumble in the bouillon cube. Cover and cook over medium-low heat until the potatoes are very soft. Pour in the milk and remaining water and bring the soup to a boil. Take off the heat and cool for 10 minutes.

Purée the soup in batches in a blender or food processor and return to the French oven. Heat the soup over low heat.

Beat the egg yolks with the sour cream, scoop into the soup, and whisk vigorously for 2 minutes.

Add salt and pepper. Keep warm over low heat, not allowing to boil, while you make the croutons.

Slice the crusts off the bread then slice into 1/2-inch (1.5-cm) or larger cubes. Heat the oil in a non-stick skillet until shimmering hot, sprinkle in 1 teaspoon salt, toss in the croutons, and fry until they are golden brown.

Ladle the soup into bowls, divide the grated radishes in the centers of each bowl and pile the croutons on top of the radishes. Drip a tiny bit of your best extra virgin olive oil in droplets around the edges to add another layer of flavor to the experience of eating this soup.

IDEAS AND SUGGESTIONS

Use a dark pumpernickel bread for the croutons instead and pulse them in the food processor so they are tiny, for a different color and kind of crunch. Fry the same way.

FIRESIDE DUCK AND CABBAGE SOUP

Soupe du Coin du Feu au Canard et au Chou SERVES 6

Very rarely it would snow at my house in the south of France. When it did, it didn't last long. So we treated it as a special occasion. We'd let the dogs out to leap around. We'd turn on the outdoor lights so we could watch the flakes spiral down. A fire would be lit. And a table would be pulled up so that we could dine in front of the fire.

I usually knew when it might snow, as the radio and newspaper would be full of warnings, and being higher up in the hills I could pretty much guess that we'd get some. So I would plan a hearty soup, more often than not a garbure *from the southwest of France, my version thick and meaty with shredded duck and loads of vegetables.*

SPECIAL EQUIPMENT 5.5-QUART (5.5-L) OR LARGER FRENCH OVEN; LARGE OVENPROOF SKILLET

4 duck breasts

Salt and pepper, to taste

2 fresh thyme stems

2 sprigs parsley

4 ounces (110 g) bacon, sliced into matchsticks

6 medium carrots, large dice

1 large yellow onion, large dice

2 stalks celery with leaves, large dice

3 medium red potatoes, large dice

1 (2-pound / 900-g) green cabbage, thinly sliced and coarsely chopped

8 cloves garlic, pressed or minced, divided (save 2 pressed cloves for bread)

2 whole cloves

1 chicken bouillon cube

5 cups (1.2 l) chicken stock

2 (16-ounce / 450-g) cans butter beans

2 tablespoons (30 ml) extra virgin olive oil

1 small baguette

PREP

Preheat the oven to 400° F (200 °C). Slash the duck skin with a sharp knife in a crisscross pattern. Season both sides with salt and pepper.

Pull the leaves from the thyme stems and discard stems. Pull parsley leaves from stems, discard stems, and mince leaves.

COOK

In the French oven, cook the bacon over medium heat until crispy. Remove with a slotted spoon to a paper towel and reserve. Leave bacon fat in the French oven.

In the ovenproof skillet, add the duck breasts, fat side down, and cook for 7 minutes, until the fat is rendered and the skin is golden brown. Turn over and cook for 2 minutes. Place in the oven and cook for 10 minutes. Remove from the oven and let rest for 5 minutes. Remove the crisp skin, coarsely chop, and reserve. Thinly slice the meat into thin shreds. Pour the duck fat into the French oven.

Add all of the vegetables into the French oven along with 6 cloves garlic, cloves, and thyme leaves then crumble in the bouillon cube. Pour in stock. Bring to a boil over medium heat, reduce to a simmer, partially cover, and cook for 30 minutes. Add the beans and cook for another 15 minutes.

Remove the cloves and discard. Add the duck meat back into the soup and stir to blend.

Slice the baguette into 6 pieces, on a diagonal, then in half horizontally. Brush with olive oil, remaining garlic, and salt and bake in the oven until golden but still soft. Sprinkle with parsley.

Serve the soup with the bacon and crispy duck skin sprinkled over the top and with a slice of garlic bread on the side.

IDEAS AND SUGGESTIONS

To make this soup true to the original recipe made in southwest France, you can purchase duck confit legs online from www.dartagnan.com.

ALSATIAN BEER AND MUNSTER SOUP

Soupe Alsacienne à la Bière et au Munster SERVES 6

Alsatian cuisine from the north of France is a Franco-German fusion, one reason why recipes from there are so interesting. Some of the dishes we are familiar with that originated in Alsace are quiche, the sweet bread kugelhopf, *and gingerbread.*

This part of France is the major producer of French beers, and during the annual beer festival they traditionally serve beer soup, sometimes made with cheese. I pair the concept with Munster cheese from Alsace because it seems natural and it melts so well onto the center of this hot soup.

Although the recipes for beer soup usually call for stale bread, I use a good-quality fresh bread, which adds another level of flavor.

SPECIAL EQUIPMENT FOOD PROCESSOR OR BLENDER; 5-QUART (5-L) OR LARGER FRENCH OVEN

6 slices good quality bread

4 tablespoons (60 g) unsalted butter, divided

1 large yellow onion, thinly sliced

4 cups (1 l) chicken stock

3 cups (700 ml) beer

¼ teaspoon freshly grated nutmeg, plus more for garnish

1½ teaspoons salt, divided

1 teaspoon freshly ground black pepper

½ cup (120 g) light cream or half-and-half

8 ounces (225 g) Munster cheese, diced (If too soft, scoop small rounds with a spoon.)

PREP

Tear up 4 slices of bread and process in food processor until finely ground (about 4 cups / 200 g). Transfer to a bowl and reserve.

Tear up remaining bread, process in food processor until finely ground, and reserve for garnish (about 2 cups / 100 g).

COOK

Melt 2 tablespoons (30 g) butter in the French oven, toss in the onion, and cook over medium heat for 7 minutes, stirring frequently.

Slowly add in the stock, beer, 4 cups (200 g) breadcrumbs, nutmeg, 1 teaspoon salt, and pepper. Bring to a boil then reduce to a simmer and cook for 15 minutes.

Meanwhile, make the breadcrumb garnish by melting remaining butter in a large skillet over medium heat. Toss in the reserved 2 cups (100 g) breadcrumbs, sprinkle with remaining salt, and fry until golden brown and crispy.

Purée half of the soup in the food processor or blender, return to the pot, and stir to combine. Whisk in the cream and heat until serving temperature.

Ladle into bowls, divide cheese onto the centers of each bowl of soup, grate nutmeg over the top, and sprinkle fried breadcrumbs in a line across the soup, from one rim to the other.

IDEAS AND SUGGESTIONS

Serve with a shaker of caraway seeds, or a small bowl of them, on the table for people to serve themselves as a garnish, if they wish. To ramp up the flavor, use rye bread or pumpernickel bread and dark beer.

VELVETY PUMPKIN PIE SOUP

Velouté Comme une Tourte au Potiron SERVES 6

Not as sweet as pumpkin pie, but with a hint of it and an echo of vanilla, my light pumpkin pie soup shines when served before a holiday turkey dinner, and equally satisfies when transformed into a main course soup served with a platter of ripe cheeses, sliced bread, and a side of seasonal salad.

SPECIAL EQUIPMENT 5-QUART (5-L) OR LARGER FRENCH OVEN; BLENDER OR FOOD PROCESSOR

3 tablespoons (45 g) unsalted butter

1 medium white onion, finely chopped

2 to 3 pounds (900 g to 1.3 kg) fresh sugar pumpkin or butternut squash, peeled and sliced into ½-inch (1.5-cm) pieces

2 medium carrots, thinly sliced

6 cups (1.5 l) chicken stock

1 teaspoon salt

3 teaspoons vanilla extract

5 tablespoons (60 g) dark brown sugar

2 teaspoons pumpkin pie spice, plus extra for garnish

1 cup (240 g) half-and-half or heavy cream

½ cup snipped chives for garnish, optional

COOK

Melt the butter in the French oven over medium heat. Add the onion and cook until transparent, about 5 minutes. Add the pumpkin, carrots, stock, and salt and bring to a boil. Reduce to a simmer and cook, uncovered, for 25 minutes or until the vegetables are very soft.

In batches, purée the soup in blender and return to the pot. Add the vanilla, brown sugar, pumpkin pie spice, and half-and-half. Whisk all together and cook until the sugar is dissolved then check for seasoning. Serve with a tiny sprinkle of pumpkin pie spice in the center of each bowl and some snipped chives for color, if you wish.

IDEAS AND SUGGESTIONS

Make your own pumpkin pie spice by mixing ground cinnamon, nutmeg, ginger, and ground cloves. Other garnishes could include crumbled bacon or chorizo, or scattered croutons and toasted pumpkin seeds.

RED CLAM SOUP WITH SALTINE CRUMB GARNISH

Soupe à la Palourde Rouge et Miettes de Crackers SERVES 6 TO 8

The saltine crumb garnish for this soup is an unexpected addition. It is a flavor bomb made with loads of garlic and parsley, which disperses into the soup as you stir it in, slightly thickening the luscious broth below. Flavor bombs are my way of boosting the experience of flavor. I make them strong and use just a little, serving more on the side for each person to add according to their taste. Most of the time I make flavor bombs in my food processor, concentrating ingredients into a highly charged paste, or, in this case, crumbs that can be layered into or sprinkled over a dish.

SPECIAL EQUIPMENT 3-QUART (3-L) OR LARGER FRENCH OVEN; FOOD PROCESSOR

- 6 tablespoons (90 ml) extra virgin olive oil, divided
- 1 medium white onion, minced
- 4 medium (2 pounds / 900 g) russet potatoes, peeled and small dice
- 6 large cloves garlic, 2 whole and 4 minced

- 1 cup (240 ml) dry white wine
- 2½ cups (600 ml) bottled clam broth
- 2½ teaspoons salt, plus ⅛ teaspoon for crumbs
- 3 (10-ounce / 280-g) cans baby clams

- 4 large unpeeled tomatoes, chopped, saving juice and seeds
- 1 (6.5-ounce / 180-g) can chopped clams, drained
- 12 saltine crackers
- 1 cup curly parsley leaves, tightly packed

COOK

In the French oven, heat 3 tablespoons (45 ml) oil over medium heat then add the onion and cook until soft, about 5 minutes.

Add the potatoes, minced garlic, wine, broth, and salt and bring to a boil over medium heat. Reduce to a simmer and cook for 12 minutes, or until the potatoes are fork tender. Add the baby clams, tomatoes with their juice and seeds, and chopped clams and simmer 10 minutes.

In the food processor, crumble in the saltines and add remaining oil, salt, parsley, and whole garlic cloves. Process until granular, ladle the soup into bowls, mound crumbs onto the center of each bowl of soup, and serve.

IDEAS AND SUGGESTIONS

To make this into a main meal, add portions of firm white fish, like halibut or cod, after you add the chopped clams. Slice the fish into as many portions as you have serving bowls of soup, so that each bowl has one portion of fish with the soup ladled over the top.

FRENCH GREEN LENTIL AND TOASTED WALNUTS SOUP

Soupe aux Lentilles Vertes du Puy et Noix Grillées SERVES 6

For such a homey soup, this surprises with its nutty flavor paired with a toasted walnut garnish. It happens because of the lentils you use, not the mushy kind, but the small green lentils du Puy from France that cook up firm, slightly peppery, and earthy in flavor, while thickening the soup enough to almost hold its shape. They can be found at many supermarkets (called French green lentils), health food stores, and at Whole Foods.

It is a good-for-you soup that is quick to prepare. Serve it with warm bread and a simple green salad for a light meal.

SPECIAL EQUIPMENT 5-QUART (5-L) OR LARGER FRENCH OVEN; FOOD PROCESSOR OR BLENDER

- 4 tablespoons (60 ml) extra virgin olive oil, divided
- 1 medium yellow onion, thinly sliced then finely chopped
- 6 medium carrots, finely diced
- 3 large cloves garlic, finely chopped
- 1 pound (450 g) lentils du Puy (small green French lentils), rinsed and drained
- 6 cups (1.5 l) chicken stock
- 1½ teaspoons salt
- 2 teaspoons coarsely ground black pepper
- 3 heaping teaspoons herbes de Provence
- 1 cup (240 ml) water
- 1 tablespoon (15 ml) red wine vinegar
- 1½ cups (150 g) shelled walnuts, finely chopped

COOK

Heat 3 tablespoons (45 ml) oil in the French oven, add the onion and carrots, and cook on medium for 6 minutes.

Add the garlic, lentils, stock, salt, pepper, and herbes de Provence. Bring to a boil then reduce to a simmer and cook, partially covered, for 25 minutes. Add water and cook another 5 minutes.

Pour half of the soup into food processor and purée. Return the purée to the French oven and stir to blend. Add remaining oil and vinegar and mix well to blend. Taste for seasoning and adjust. Add a bit more water if the soup is too thick.

In a large skillet over medium-high heat, toast the walnuts. Ladle the soup into bowls and divide the toasted walnuts onto the centers of each bowl of soup.

IDEAS AND SUGGESTIONS

A final drizzle of great olive oil brings out the complexity of the flavors in this soup. You can also grate Parmesan cheese over the top to melt into the soup for a heartier version.

RIES VAN NOTEN   7

CAFE DES BEAUX ARTS

CAFE

BREAKFAST

RUE
BONAPAR

RUE
BONAPAR

CAFÉ

BAKING

There are so many reasons to bake in a French oven. The most important for me is that French ovens themselves act like a small oven, the inside being surrounded by thick walls emanating a uniform heat. They are superb at baking with the cover on, especially for breads. Because they trap moisture from dough and retain the heat, you can produce homemade bread with a beautiful crisp crust. Professional bakers use steam in their ovens for a shiny crisp crust, but baking in a French oven does pretty close to the same thing. For the same reason, you can quickly bake a divine pizza. I keep two dedicated French ovens just for this kind of covered baking, so I can make two loaves of bread or two pizzas at a time.

You can bake almost anything in a French oven. Your imagination is the only limit. The following recipes will give you an idea of the kind of dishes you can bake then bring to the table without transferring to a serving dish.

Note: If your French oven does not have one, purchase a metal knob for it to use when baking with its lid on at higher temperatures.

HOMEMADE BASIL GARLIC BREAD

Pain Maison à l'Ail et au Basilic MAKES 1 LOAF

Depending on how you treat the top before you put it in the oven, your bread will take on different looks. For this one, I cut a small cross in the center before baking it so that it opened up in the middle as it baked. Sometimes I do not cut the top of the dough at all, and let the green of the basil ooze out where it may. And sometimes I slash three deep cuts from side to side, so the bread opens out more like an accordion.

At first, this recipe will seem like a lot of steps, but after you do it once, it will all make sense and the next time you make bread it will move more quickly and intuitively.

SPECIAL EQUIPMENT PARCHMENT PAPER; 4-QUART (4-L) OR LARGER FRENCH OVEN; FOOD PROCESSOR

Bread

1 cup (240 ml) warm water

1 teaspoon sugar

1 package active dry yeast

3 cups (360 g) bread flour, plus more if needed

1½ teaspoons kosher or sea salt

1 large egg, beat with 1 teaspoon water

3 tablespoons (45 g) butter, melted

Filling

2 cloves garlic

1 bunch fresh basil

½ teaspoon kosher or sea salt

4 ounces (110 g) Parmesan cheese, sliced

2 tablespoons (30 ml) extra virgin olive oil, divided

PREP

Place a shelf in the middle of your oven. Cut a piece of parchment paper larger than your French oven that is big enough to hold the dough and act as a sling when you lower it into the French oven. Butter the bottom only of the French oven.

COOK

Bread

Place the water and sugar into a small bowl and stir until the sugar dissolves. Sprinkle the yeast over the top and let set for 10–15 minutes, until the mixture looks foamy.

Meanwhile, add the flour and salt to the food processor.

When the yeast mixture is foamy, turn on the food processor and pour in the yeast mixture and the egg until it forms a dough ball. Pour in the melted butter, and process for 5–10 seconds, until a ball reforms.

Preheat the oven to 350° F (180 °C) for only 2 minutes then turn off the oven. This will warm it up enough to put the dough in to rise.

Turn out the dough into a large oiled bowl, rolling it around to coat with oil, and cover with plastic wrap. Place a towel over the top. Put it in the oven with the door shut and leave for 1½ hours, until dough doubles in size.

Filling

While the dough is rising, make the filling. With the food processor running, toss in the garlic to mince. Turn off the machine, add the basil, salt, and Parmesan and process for 20 seconds. With the machine running, pour in 1 tablespoon (15 ml) oil and process until mixture is smooth.

After 1½ hours, take the bowl of dough out of the oven.

Put the French oven into your oven and preheat to 450° F (230° C) for 35 minutes.

continued >

Meanwhile, turn the dough out onto a clean, well-floured work surface. Flour your hands and gently roll out the dough to a little larger than the size of your French oven. Spread the filling over it to within ¼ inch (.5 cm) of the sides, roll up the dough, and bring it together into a ball. Pinch the seams to seal and place the dough on the center of the parchment paper, seam side down.

With kitchen mitts, carefully lift the French oven out of the hot oven and place it on a kitchen towel or heat-proof surface.

Hold both sides of the parchment paper and use it like a sling to lower dough into the hot French oven. Put the lid on, with parchment paper hanging outside, and place the French oven on the middle rack of the oven. Bake for 30 minutes. Take the lid off and see if it is browned and cooked through. I usually stop at this point, but if yours needs added browning or cooking, keep it uncovered and cook in the oven an additional 5–10 minutes.

Remove from the oven and allow the bread to cool at least 10 minutes before slicing.

IDEAS AND SUGGESTIONS

Some other additions that might be tasty are, herbs and oil-cured black olives; green olives and cheese; raisins and chopped walnuts, sunflower seeds, orange, and cranberries.

DATE AND RAISIN SODA BREAD

Soda Bread aux Dattes et aux Raisins secs MAKES 1 LOAF

One of the most memorable breakfasts I have ever had was at a small hotel in Burgundy where the owner had walked out into his vineyard and picked a small cluster of grapes, which were put on a plate before me with the morning dew still clinging to them. Beside them was a basket with warm raisin walnut rolls cuddled in a crisp white napkin and a plate with curls of sweet butter. That memory and those rolls encouraged me to create a similar recipe, which over the years morphed into this rustic date and raisin soda bread that I make in a French oven.

It is easy and quick enough to make in time for breakfast. Just make sure to buy chopped dates, which are coated and won't clump in the batter.

SPECIAL EQUIPMENT 4.5- TO 5-QUART (4.5- TO 5-L) FRENCH OVEN

3 cups (360 g) all-purpose flour

1 cup (120 g) bread flour

½ teaspoon ground cinnamon

1½ teaspoons baking soda

½ teaspoon baking powder

1 teaspoon kosher or sea salt

3 tablespoons (35 g) dark brown sugar

3 tablespoons (45 g) butter, chilled

1 large egg, room temperature

1½ cups (360 ml) buttermilk

1 cup (175 g) chopped dates

½ cup (75 g) raisins

1 tablespoon (15 g) butter, melted for brushing the top

PREP

Preheat oven to 400° F (200° C) and butter the bottom of the French oven.

COOK

Sift the flours, cinnamon, baking soda, baking powder, and salt together into a large bowl. Whisk in the brown sugar. Slice in the butter and work it into the dough with a pastry cutter or with your fingers by rubbing and pinching the flour together until well blended. (You can alternatively do this step by putting the dry ingredients into a food processor, slicing in the butter, and pulsing until well blended).

Beat the egg into the buttermilk, pour into the bowl, and mix with a fork until thoroughly blended. Add the dates and raisins and mix again until it all starts to come together.

Scoop the dough onto a clean floured work surface and bring it together into a round that will fit into your French oven. Do not knead the dough, as it will make it tough. Just work it enough to bring it into a cohesive, slightly flattened round.

Slice a deep crisscross with a small sharp knife on the top of the dough.

Lower into the French oven, cover with the lid, place in the oven, and bake for 20 minutes. Take the lid off, brush with the melted butter, and bake until the loaf is a beautiful golden brown, about 20–25 minutes. It will be done when a cake tester comes out clean.

Remove from the oven and allow to rest for 15 minutes. Lift the bread out of the French oven with a spatula and place it on a cutting board. Use a serrated bread knife to slice.

IDEAS AND SUGGESTIONS

If you don't have buttermilk at hand, make it as follows: ½ tablespoon white vinegar in ½ cup (120 ml) milk to make ½ cup buttermilk.

Sprinkle bottom of French oven with coarse cornmeal before placing the bread in it to bake.

SUPER CREAMY GOAT CHEESE VEGETABLE LASAGNA

Lasagnes Super-Crémeuses aux Légumes et au Fromage de Chèvre SERVES 6

Where I lived in Bar-sur-Loup, along the Riviera, the local cheese culture was one of owning a few goats, making cheese, and hanging a sign out along the road to sell it. This was heavenly for me to drive along the back roads on my way somewhere and pass by inviting hand-lettered signs. I inevitably stopped and bought some, as each homemade cheese was individual in the way it tasted depending on what the goats were grazing on.

Once I had an abundance of goat cheese, I would make this lasagna. There are three steps: making the tomato layer; the ricotta cheese layer; and the béchamel sauce layer. Once these are done, assembling the lasagna takes only a few minutes before you can put it in the oven to bake.

SPECIAL EQUIPMENT FOOD PROCESSOR; 5-QUART (5-L) FRENCH OVEN; KITCHEN SCISSORS

Tomato Layer

1 small yellow onion, peeled and sliced into big chunks

2 large cloves garlic

3 Roma tomatoes, cut into thirds

2 teaspoons sugar

¼ teaspoon crushed red pepper flakes

1 (8.5-ounce / 250-g) jar sun-dried tomatoes, drained

Ricotta Layer

1 (32-ounce / 900-g) container whole-milk ricotta cheese

2 large eggs, beaten

1 tablespoon extra virgin olive oil

½ teaspoon salt

½ teaspoon coarsely ground black pepper

1 medium zucchini, grated and squeezed very dry

1 medium carrot, grated

¼ cup (15 g) minced fresh basil leaves

2 large cloves garlic, pressed or minced

Béchamel Layer

¼ cup (60 g) unsalted butter

¼ cup (30 g) all-purpose flour

2 cups (480 ml) milk

8 ounces (225 g) soft goat cheese

⅛ teaspoon cayenne pepper

1 teaspoon salt

1 pound (450 g) fresh lasagna sheets

8 ounces (225 g) fresh mozzarella, grated on the large holes of a box grater and divided into thirds

COOK

Tomato Layer

Place the onion, garlic, and tomatoes into the food processor and add the sugar, red pepper flakes, and sun-dried tomatoes. Process until smooth, but still with some texture.

Ricotta Layer

In a large bowl, mix the ingredients together with a fork until well combined.

Béchamel Layer

In a large saucepan, melt butter with the flour while whisking and cooking for about 2 minutes. Slowly add milk while whisking. Bring to a simmer, whisk until the sauce is thick and coats the back of a spoon, then slice in the goat cheese, stir until it has completely melted, add the cayenne and salt, and stir well to combine.

Preheat the oven to 375° F (190° C).

Assemble the lasagna by ladling a ^{1}/4 cup (60 ml) of the béchamel sauce into the French oven. Cut the fresh lasagna sheets with scissors to fit and make a layer in the French oven. They can be sliced in quarters and patch-worked in. It doesn't matter if there are some small gaps or that it doesn't look perfect.

Spoon on and spread ^{1}/2 cup (120 ml) of the ricotta mixture over the pasta. Sprinkle on a third of the mozzarella. Add a pasta layer, then ^{3}/4 cup (180 ml) of the tomato mixture, then pasta, then ^{3}/4 cup (180 ml) ricotta. Sprinkle another third of the mozzarella over the top. Add another pasta layer, then ^{1}/2 cup (120 ml) béchamel, then pasta, then ^{3}/4 cups (180 ml) tomato mixture. Sprinkle on the remaining mozzarella.

From here on, layer according to how much you have left of every ingredient. You want to end up with the top layer being ^{3}/4 cup (180 ml) of the tomato mixture topped with ^{1}/2 cup (120 ml) to ^{3}/4 cup (180 ml) of the béchamel.

Cover and bake in the oven for 35–40 minutes. Remove from oven, remove the cover, and let the lasagna set for 15 minutes before serving.

IDEAS AND SUGGESTIONS

If you use no-boil dried lasagna noodles instead, break them up to fit into layers in the French oven. It will give it a rustic look. Also check their cooking time on the back of the package.

You can skip the béchamel layer to speed up the process, but I just love its creaminess in my lasagna.

The tomato sauce and ricotta mixture can be done a day ahead and refrigerated. Or you can assemble the entire lasagna, cover it, and refrigerate to bake it the next day. Bring to room temperature before putting it in the oven.

LAMB HACHIS PARMENTIER

Hachis Parmentier d'Agneau SERVES 6

In the latter part of the eighteenth century, Antoine-Augustin Parmentier came up with a dish to promote potatoes as a cash crop and one that could feed the population of France. The previously scorned potato, considered only fit for feeding cattle, was transformed by his efforts into being seen as appropriate for human consumption. The dish he created, and which was named after him, is one of the most popular casseroles you will find in family homes in France. At about the same time in England, a similar effort was being made to promote the lowly potato and the English version was called cottage pie, or shepherd's pie. Both have a layer of meat at the bottom with a topping of fluffy mashed potatoes.

The word hachis *refers to a dish where the meat is finely chopped. I chop mine in a food processor to obtain finely chopped lamb, rather than using ready-ground lamb, because I prefer the texture. Ask your butcher for lamb top round, a cut similar to beef sirloin, if you are going to grind it yourself.*

SPECIAL EQUIPMENT FOOD PROCESSOR; WAX OR PARCHMENT PAPER; 5-QUART (5-L) OR LARGER FRENCH OVEN; STAND MIXER; BAKING SHEET

- 2 fresh thyme sprigs
- 1 fresh rosemary sprig
- 2½ to 3 pounds (1.1 kg to 1.4 kg) russet potatoes, peeled and sliced into 1-inch (2.5-cm) cubes
- 1 heaping tablespoon salt
- 2 pounds (900 g) lamb top round, fat and sinew trimmed off and sliced into 1-inch (2.5-cm) cubes
- 2 tablespoons (15 g) all-purpose flour, plus extra

- 1 teaspoon kosher or sea salt
- 1 teaspoon coarsely ground black pepper
- 4 ounces (110 g) bacon, cut into ½-inch (1.5-cm) pieces
- 2 tablespoons (30 ml) extra virgin olive oil, divided
- 1 medium yellow onion, finely chopped
- 2 medium carrots, cut into small dice
- 5 large cloves garlic, pressed or finely chopped

- 1 beef bouillon cube
- ¾ cup (180 ml) dry red wine
- 1 (14-ounce / 400-g) jar pizza sauce
- 1 cup (150 g) frozen baby peas
- ¾ cup (180 g) half-and-half
- 2 tablespoons (30 g) unsalted butter
- ½ teaspoon salt
- 4 tablespoons (25 g) finely grated Pecorino Romano cheese

PREP

Preheat the oven to 400° F (200° C). Pull leaves from thyme and rosemary. Discard stems. Finely chop the herbs and mix together.

COOK

Put the potatoes into a large saucepan, cover with water, add 1 heaping tablespoon salt, bring to a boil, reduce to a simmer, and cook until tender, about 10–12 minutes. Drain in a colander and allow to cool so that the steam is released and the potatoes dry out.

Place lamb in the food processor in batches and process each batch for about 10 seconds, until you have minced meat that still has texture and is not ground. Lay out a large piece of wax or parchment paper on a work surface, scoop the lamb onto the paper and spread it out. Sprinkle with the flour, salt, and pepper and toss with a fork to coat.

In the French oven, add the bacon and cook on medium until crispy. Remove to paper towels and reserve. Leave the bacon fat in the French oven. Heat the bacon fat up to shimmering hot, over medium heat, then toss in half the lamb and cook until browned. Remove to large bowl and repeat with remaining lamb.

Add 1 tablespoon (15 ml) oil to the French oven then add the onion, carrots, and garlic. Crumble in the bouillon cube. Cook on medium, stirring frequently, for 5 minutes.

Add the lamb back into the French oven then add the wine, pizza sauce, thyme, and rosemary and stir. Cook on medium heat for 4 minutes. Stir in the peas and reserved bacon and keep at a low simmer until ready to bake.

Heat the half-and-half, butter, remaining oil, and salt in a small saucepan.

Toss the potatoes into the stand mixer (if you have a potato ricer, put them through it and beat with a wooden spoon), and begin to break them down. Slowly pour in the hot half-and-half mixture, stopping halfway to see how the texture is. Use only as much as you need of the remaining liquid to beat the potatoes to the consistency you like. Taste for seasoning and adjust.

Place the French oven on the baking sheet (since it could bubble over), spread the mashed potatoes over the top, sprinkle on the cheese, place in the oven, and bake for 15–20 minutes, until bubbling hot and turning golden on the top.

EASY PIZZA FOR TWO

Pizza Facile pour Deux SERVES 2

French ovens make the best pizza ever, giving them a marvelous crust. I make this pizza recipe for two, but you can also slice it into 6 pieces to serve with wine for a snack before dinner.

It couldn't be easier. First, buy a ball of dough from your local pizza shop and tell them you want one for a small-size pizza. Take it home, cover it, and leave it on the counter until ready to use. Once you see how quick and easy this pizza is to make, you'll want to make it again and again with whatever toppings you are in the mood for. I often make this with anchovies and oil-cured black olives, and after it comes out of the oven, I grate sharp Parmigiano-Reggiano all over the top.

In fact, pulling this together goes so quickly that you can remove the pizza to a cutting board, leave the oven on, fit in another disk of pizza dough, arrange toppings, cook it for 3 minutes on top of the stove, and pop it in the oven for another round that will be ready in 14 minutes.

SPECIAL EQUIPMENT BOX GRATER; 5-QUART (5-L) OR LARGER FRENCH OVEN

8 ounces (225 g) fresh mozzarella

3 tablespoons (45 ml) extra virgin olive oil

¼ small onion, sliced very thinly

2 cloves garlic, pressed or minced

½ teaspoon salt

1 ball pizza dough for a small pizza purchased from your local pizza shop

4 tablespoons (60 ml) canned or bottled pizza sauce

1 heaping tablespoon herbes de Provence

8 fresh basil leaves, torn

3 ounces (90 g) prosciutto

3 ounces (90 g) Parmesan cheese

PREP

Preheat oven to 425° F (220° C). Grate half the mozzarella on the large holes of a box grater. Slice the rest into big pieces.

COOK

Heat the oil in the French oven over medium heat, toss in the onion, garlic, and salt, and cook until the onion slices are tender, about 6 minutes.

With a slotted spoon, scoop out the onion mixture to a plate and reserve, leaving the oil at the bottom. The onions and garlic will have flavored the oil and will flavor the underside of the pizza.

When the French oven is cooler and can be touched, place the pizza dough into the bottom over the oil, and stretch it out to fit, bringing up a slight rim around the sides.

Spread the pizza sauce over the dough and spoon on the cooked onions and garlic. Sprinkle with the herbes de Provence and basil, arrange slices of mozzarella and prosciutto all over, distribute the grated mozzarella, and then grate the Parmesan to finish.

Place the French oven on the stovetop, cover with its lid, and cook over medium high heat for 3 minutes.

Remove the lid, place in the oven, and bake for 14 minutes, until crisp and golden.

Remove the pizza from the oven. With a fork, gently coax up the edges then, with a spatula, lift the whole pizza to a cutting board. Slice and serve.

IDEAS AND SUGGESTIONS

Fry pepperoni slices in the oil, remove to a plate, and fit the pizza dough over the pepperoni-flavored oil in the French oven for an incredibly delicious crust. Use the pepperoni slices for the top of the pie.

CAULIFLOWER AND VERY ARTICHOKE GRATIN

Gratin de Chou-Fleur aux Artichauts SERVES 6

I was visiting an open-air market in Provence and happened upon the most beautiful purple-blue flowers. I was told they were blooming artichokes, which happens when the buds are allowed to open and flower. I didn't know until they told me that artichokes are the unopened flowers of a thistle. Suddenly I felt a deeper connection to an ingredient I used so frequently without thinking about anything other than its flavor.

The combination of cauliflower and artichokes in this recipe happened because I had them both on hand on the day I was in the mood for making a big, homey casserole-type dish in a French oven that I wanted to bring to a party. It has lots of cheese in it as well, providing a lovely texture and flavor boost.

SPECIAL EQUIPMENT 5-QUART (5-L) OR LARGER FRENCH OVEN; FOOD PROCESSOR

1 (3- to 3½-pound / 1.3- kg to 1.6-kg) head cauliflower

3 large cloves garlic, divided

2 (6-ounce / 170-g) jars marinated artichoke hearts

2 (14-ounce / 400-g) cans quartered artichoke hearts

4 tablespoons (60 g) unsalted butter, softened

4 tablespoons (30 g) all-purpose flour

2 cups (480 ml) milk, room temperature

1 chicken or vegetable bouillon cube

2 teaspoons Dijon mustard

1 cup (100 g) grated Parmesan cheese

8 ounces (225 g) fontina cheese, coarsely grated

Topping

½ cup (50 g) grated Parmesan cheese

½ cup (40 g) panko breadcrumbs

4 tablespoons (60 ml) extra virgin olive oil

PREP

Preheat oven to 375° F (190° C).

Cut florets off the cauliflower (about 5 heaping cups), trying to keep them the same size so that they cook uniformly, and slice away the stems. Discard the core and stems or use for soup.

Slice 1 clove garlic in half and rub French oven with the halves.

In the food processor, purée jars of the marinated artichoke hearts, including liquid from 1 jar, with 2 cloves garlic and the halves rubbed on French oven.

Drain the cans of quartered artichoke hearts. Squeeze very dry in paper towels.

COOK

To make a Mornay sauce, melt the butter in the French oven, sprinkle in the flour, and whisk for 2 minutes while cooking. Very slowly add in the milk while whisking to combine. Add the bouillon cube and mustard. Continue cooking and whisking until the sauce is thickened. Add the Parmesan and fontina cheeses, puréed artichoke hearts, and canned artichoke quarters and stir to combine.

Stir in the cauliflower florets to completely coat and bake in the oven for 30–40 minutes, until the cauliflower is tender and to your liking. You can bake it longer to get a softer texture.

Topping

Toss the Parmesan, panko crumbs, and oil to coat. Spread the crumb topping over the top, place back in the oven, and bake for 15–20 minutes until it is bubbling and golden on top. Cool 10 minutes before serving.

IDEAS AND SUGGESTIONS

Try replacing the cheeses with Gruyère or sharp cheddar. Add thinly sliced leeks and Brussels sprouts leaves, or leave out cauliflower and use broccoli instead. Mash leftovers the next day.

RED PEPPER, POTATO, AND TOMATO CASSEROLE

Casserole de Poivron Rouge, Pomme de Terre et Tomate SERVES 6

After fishing in the river below our house, and being one of the first I had ever heard of to actually catch a fish in it, our friend decided to celebrate by preparing his fish for our dinner. I offered to cook a side dish and climbed up to my garden on the hill to see what I could find to work with. Basket full, I returned to the kitchen and, while he gutted and cleaned his magnificent catch, I put this casserole together and set it in the oven to bake.

We liked it enough that it became a no-thought addition to many meals. It works beautifully when prepared in a French oven.

SPECIAL EQUIPMENT 5-QUART (5-L) FRENCH OVEN

- 6 large cloves garlic, 1 clove sliced in half and others finely chopped
- 3 medium Yukon gold potatoes, peeled and sliced ⅛ inch (½ cm) thick then sliced into half moons
- 3 teaspoons salt, divided
- 3 tablespoons (45 ml) extra virgin olive oil, plus extra

- 1 medium red onion, finely chopped
- 3 medium to large red bell peppers, sliced into ½-inch (1.5-cm) wide pieces
- 2 tablespoons (30 ml) red wine vinegar
- 2 teaspoons sugar
- 3 tablespoons (45 ml) dry white wine
- 1 chicken bouillon cube

- ½ teaspoon Dijon mustard
- A few cracks of coarsely ground pepper
- ½ tablespoon fresh or dried thyme leaves
- 4 plum tomatoes, sliced
- 1 small red onion, sliced into thin half moons
- ¼ cup (25 g) grated Parmesan cheese

PREP

Preheat oven to 350° F (180° C). Rub the sliced garlic over the bottom and sides of the French oven.

COOK

Place potatoes in a large saucepan and cover with water. Add 2 teaspoons salt, cover, bring to a boil, uncover, reduce to a simmer, and cook for 2 minutes. Drain into a colander.

In the French oven, heat the oil over medium heat, sprinkle in remaining salt, add the chopped onion and bell peppers, and cook for 7 minutes, stirring frequently.

Mix the vinegar and sugar together and pour into the French oven. Add half of the garlic, stir to combine, and cook another 2 minutes. Arrange the potatoes over the red peppers.

In a small bowl, add the wine, grate in the bouillon cube, add the mustard and the remaining garlic, and mix well to combine. Pour the wine mixture over the potatoes and add a few cracks of coarsely ground black pepper and the thyme.

Arrange the sliced tomatoes over the potatoes, drizzle with olive oil, scatter the sliced red onion over the top and sprinkle with the cheese. Cover and bake for 30 minutes.

IDEAS AND SUGGESTIONS

You can flake in a layer of cod on top of the red pepper layer for a lovely fish dinner.

STOVETOP

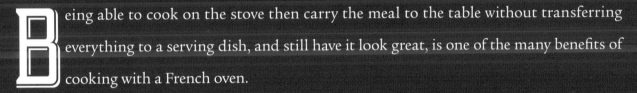eing able to cook on the stove then carry the meal to the table without transferring everything to a serving dish, and still have it look great, is one of the many benefits of cooking with a French oven.

Simmering soups, poached fish, quick one-pot pastas, one-meal risottos, stews, curries, and chili are all so much more satisfying than when made in other pots and pans. For me, there is no comparison. And made in a French oven, everything looks special.

SUPER MOIST OLIVE OIL-POACHED SALMON AND MEYER LEMONS

Saumon Confit à l'Huile d'Olive et aux Citrons Meyer SERVES 4

This recipe makes the most spectacular fish I have ever eaten. It comes out super moist and tender due to the technique of poaching the fish at a very low temperature, submerged in olive oil. It is basically a confit. (A confit is a French cooking term that refers to a technique of cooking meat, poultry, or fish in fat or oil at a very low temperature.) Use a good olive oil as it goes so well with fish, adds flavor, and because both are a traditional pair in healthy Mediterranean cooking.

We took the picture so that you could see what it looks like just before cooking the salmon. I use about 4 cups of extra virgin olive oil. I then save it to use again for shrimp or seafood later in the week. After cooking and cooling the oil to room temperature, I strain it through cheesecloth and keep it in the refrigerator in a screw-top jar. It lasts for a couple of weeks.

Prepare some couscous at the same time in a saucepan next to your French oven and you have a deliriously delicious meal in well under 30 minutes.

SPECIAL EQUIPMENT 5-QUART (5-L) FRENCH OVEN; CANDY OR FRYING THERMOMETER

Salmon

4 cups (1 l) olive oil

2 teaspoons salt, plus more, divided

1 tablespoon crushed pink peppercorns

⅛ teaspoon cayenne pepper

1 teaspoon dried thyme

2 medium Meyer lemons, 1 sliced into thin half moons and 1 quartered

2 large cloves garlic, thinly sliced

2 bay leaves, broken into small pieces

4 (5-ounce / 140-g) salmon filets, the same thickness so they cook evenly

2 tablespoons capers

Couscous

1¼ cup (300 ml) water

1 cup (180 g) couscous

1 pint (280 g) cherry tomatoes, sliced in half lengthwise

1 ripe avocado, peeled and sliced into small dice

¼ small red onion, diced

2 tablespoons (30 ml) extra virgin olive oil

3 teaspoons (15 ml) red wine vinegar

¼ teaspoon salt

COOK

Salmon

Pour the oil into the French oven; add the salt, peppercorns, cayenne, thyme, slices of lemon, garlic, and bay leaves and heat on low to barely a simmer, around 140° F (60° C) on the thermometer, letting the ingredients cook in the oil for 15 minutes.

Liberally salt the salmon filets before submerging them into the oil. Cook, covered, on low heat for anywhere from 9–17 minutes, depending on their thickness. Thinner filets could take as little as 5 minutes, thicker from 10–17, so keep watch. Slice into the middle of 1 filet to check that it is done to your taste. If it needs to cook longer, keep the filets in the hot oil for another 3 minutes.

Couscous

Meanwhile, make the couscous by boiling the water in a saucepan. Pour in the couscous, cover, and remove from the heat. After 4 minutes, uncover and fluff with a fork. Toss in the tomatoes, avocado, and onion. Combine the oil, vinegar, and salt and pour in the pan and mix with a fork to coat.

To serve, transfer the salmon to paper towels to drain. Place a piece of salmon on each plate, drizzle with a little of the poaching liquid, top with pieces of poached lemon, and scatter capers around. Spoon a mound of couscous to the side and lean a wedge of lemon into the couscous.

THICK ALSATIAN PORK CHOPS WITH GINGERSNAP GRAVY

Côtes de Porc à l'Alsacienne, Sauce au Pain d'Épice SERVES 4

Alsace is known for its gingerbread called pain d'épice, *and some people there prepare a recipe of sliced roasted pork with a gingerbread sauce that I've always found intriguing. Since I don't always have gingerbread, I substitute gingersnap cookies, which gives almost the same effect, and I've paired it here with large juicy pork chops and egg noodles.*

SPECIAL EQUIPMENT 5-QUART (5-L) OR LARGER FRENCH OVEN; LARGE OVENPROOF SKILLET OR GRILL PAN; MEAT THERMOMETER

4 thick pork chops, room temperature

Salt and pepper, to season pork chops

3 tablespoons (45 ml) olive oil

1 large onion, finely chopped

1 teaspoon salt

6 gingersnap cookies, crushed

1 (16-ounce / 475-ml) bottle dark beer

¼ teaspoon ground ginger

1 tablespoon (15 g) plus 1 teaspoon sugar

4 cracks coarsely ground black pepper

½ teaspoon cinnamon

2 tablespoons (30 g) heavy cream

Cooked egg noodles

PREP

Preheat the oven to 450° F (230° C). Rinse and pat dry the pork chops. Generously salt and pepper both sides.

COOK

In the French oven, heat the oil then add the onion and salt and cook on medium for 7 minutes. Add the gingersnaps, beer, ground ginger, sugar, pepper, and cinnamon. Bring to a boil over medium heat, reduce to a simmer, and cook for 10 minutes. Whisk to smooth the gravy.

Whisk in cream. Taste for seasoning and add salt and more pepper, if desired. Keep warm while you cook the pork chops.

Oil the ovenproof skillet and heat it until it is very hot. Cook the pork chops until they take on a beautiful golden color. Place in the oven for anywhere from 5–10 minutes. Timing will depend on the thickness of your chops, but you want them to be cooked through and no longer pink. Insert the meat thermometer into the thickest part of the chops and take them out when they reach 135° F (57° C). Let the chops rest for 10 minutes after removing from oven.

Mound a heap of noodles in the center of each plate and tip a pork chop over one side. Ladle gravy over the noodles only and serve with a pitcher of extra gravy on the table.

IDEAS AND SUGGESTIONS

Add a splash of cognac or brandy before adding the cream.

MUSHROOM AND FRESH HERBES DE PROVENCE RISOTTO

Risotto aux Champignons et aux Herbes de Provence SERVES 4 TO 6

When I lived in the south of France, I used Camargue rice to make risotto. It is a short-grain rice with a dark color and earthy flavor from the region around Arles in Provence. I also liked to make it with creamy Carnaroli rice from the nearby Piedmonte region of Italy.

My village was close to Nice, in a region that was part of Italy until 1860. Risotto was on many restaurant menus and you might find anything mixed into it, from truffles, to foie gras and fresh figs, to chanterelles. My Italian girlfriend in the next village even made hers with strawberries from her garden topped with shards of salty sharp Parmigiano-Reggiano.

I eventually settled on this simple recipe for risotto with mushrooms and fresh herbes de Provence. It pairs beautifully with a grilled steak or roast chicken.

SPECIAL EQUIPMENT 5-QUART (5-L) OR LARGER FRENCH OVEN

- 2 sprigs fresh marjoram
- 2 sprigs fresh rosemary
- 2 sprigs fresh thyme
- 6 tablespoons (90 ml) extra virgin olive oil, divided
- 1½ teaspoons kosher salt, divided

- 16 ounces (450 g) white button mushrooms, cleaned and thickly sliced
- 7 large cloves garlic, minced, divided
- 4½ cups (1.1 l) chicken or vegetable stock

- 1 small yellow onion, finely chopped
- 1½ cups (300 g) risotto or Arborio rice
- 1 cup (240 ml) dry white wine
- 5 ounces (140 g) grated Parmigiano-Reggiano cheese
- Coarsely ground black pepper

PREP

Pull leaves off marjoram, rosemary, and thyme. Finely chop rosemary leaves.

COOK

In a large skillet, heat 3 tablespoons (45 ml) oil and ½ teaspoon salt until shimmering hot. Toss in all of the mushrooms and 3 cloves minced garlic and stir. Cook over medium heat until the mushrooms lose their moisture and are golden and caramelized. Remove from the heat and reserve, uncovered.

Heat the stock in a saucepan and keep it hot and ready to use. Place a ladle nearby.

Heat remaining oil in the French oven over medium heat then toss in the onion and cook for 5 minutes. Add remaining minced garlic and cook for 2 minutes. Add the rice and stir. Pour in the wine and simmer, stirring once in a while until it is almost evaporated. Ladle in 1 cup (240 ml) hot stock, simmer and stir once in a while, until the liquid is almost evaporated. Repeat with the remaining stock, ½ cup (120 ml) at a time, until the rice is cooked and the stock used up, about 20 minutes.

Turn off the heat and stir in remaining salt and the cheese. Taste and add more salt and lots of coarsely ground pepper, if desired, stirring to combine. Cover and let the risotto set for 3 minutes.

Spoon the risotto onto plates. Divide the reserved mushrooms over the top of each plate. Scatter the marjoram, thyme, and chopped rosemary around the mushrooms like a wreath and serve.

IDEAS AND SUGGESTIONS

Take a little longer in the beginning by caramelizing, in separate batches, the sliced onions as well as the mushrooms. Then stir them in at the end. I sometimes use finely chopped pears instead of mushrooms, sautéing them in butter and topping the risotto with them.

ONE-POT NIÇOISE PASTA

Pâtes à la Niçoise SERVES 6

I wanted to show you this technique for cooking pasta in a French oven because you don't need a pot of boiling water to cook the pasta and another pot to cook the sauce. You can cook the pasta all at once in the French oven and carry it to the table to serve from. This is a true one-pot meal that is quick and delicious.

I use a flavor bomb (creating a strongly flavored paste) in this recipe. First, you will cook the pasta in wine and chicken stock rather than water to produce a much more flavorful pasta. Then, you will make a flavor bomb from tuna, anchovies, hot pepper flakes, and garlic. Once the pasta is cooked, you mix it in just before serving.

Personalize this recipe by creating your own version of a flavor bomb, or by simply stirring in a jar of marinara sauce at the end. Quick and simple.

SPECIAL EQUIPMENT FOOD PROCESSOR; 5-QUART (5-L) FRENCH OVEN

4 tablespoons (60 ml) extra virgin olive oil, divided

2 (5-ounce / 140-g) cans tuna in olive oil, drained

1 can anchovies in oil, drained

5 large cloves garlic

3 teaspoons Dijon mustard

1 medium organic lemon, zested and ½ juiced

1 medium yellow onion, finely chopped

1 pound (450 g) uncooked medium shells or short rigatoni pasta (or any dried short pasta)

3 cups (720 ml) dry white wine

3 cups (720 ml) chicken stock

1 teaspoon salt

¼ teaspoon hot pepper flakes

⅓ cup (35 g) freshly grated Parmesan cheese

1 pint (280 g) cherry tomatoes, sliced in half lengthwise

½ cup (15 g) tightly packed fresh basil leaves, coarsely chopped

COOK

Place 2 tablespoons (30 ml) oil, tuna, anchovies, garlic, mustard, and lemon zest into the food processor and process until well blended. This is your flavor bomb.

In the French oven, heat remaining oil over medium heat, add the onion and cook for 5 minutes. Add the pasta, wine, stock, salt, and hot pepper flakes and bring to a boil over medium heat. Reduce to a simmer, cover, and cook for 7 minutes or until the pasta is cooked to your liking.

Stir in the contents of the food processor and the lemon juice and continually stir over the heat for

a couple of minutes so that it becomes a bit creamy in texture and everything blends well. Add the cheese and stir until it melts and blends in. Taste for seasoning and add salt or pepper. If you would like the pasta moister, juice the remaining lemon and add in, or add ¼ cup (60 ml) or more of wine or chicken stock and stir well to blend.

Add the tomatoes and basil and stir to combine. Serve immediately.

IDEAS AND SUGGESTIONS

In the summer, make this recipe in the French oven then chill it in the refrigerator and serve it cold.

SOFT PARMESAN POLENTA WITH ARUGULA SALAD AND POACHED EGG

Polenta Moelleuse au Parmesan, Salade de Roquette et Oeuf Poché SERVES 4

The Niçois prepare yellow cornmeal in various ways, making it into panisses or into soft polenta. It's one of the ultimate comfort foods for me—the texture on my tongue, the flavor, the warmth, all being irresistible.

I cook mine in chicken stock and milk, stir it frequently, hover over it a bit, cook it for a little over half the time prescribed on the package because I like a bit of bite to mine, and, in between stirrings, I set the table, uncork the wine, and make the salad.

Recipe note: Depending upon the brand and grind of the cornmeal you buy, cornmeal to liquid ratios may differ, so follow the directions on the back of the package for wet ratio to dry ingredients. Feel free to stop cooking when it reaches a consistency and bite you like. I use Bob's Red Mill Corn Grits/Polenta for this recipe (available online and in health and gourmet stores). Although Bob's package instructs to cook it for 30 minutes, I cook mine for anywhere from 15–20 minutes.

SPECIAL EQUIPMENT 4.5-QUART (4.5-L) OR LARGER FRENCH OVEN

Vinaigrette

⅛ cup (30 ml) extra virgin olive oil

½ teaspoon Dijon mustard

1 teaspoon white wine vinegar

Pinch of salt

Pinch of pepper

Polenta

4 cups (960 ml) water, plus ¾ cup (180 ml) more, divided

2 cups (480 ml) milk

4 chicken bouillon cubes

¼ teaspoon ground white pepper

⅛ teaspoon cayenne pepper

1 teaspoon Dijon mustard

2 cups (340 g) cornmeal/polenta

1 tablespoon (15 g) unsalted butter

¼ cup (25 g) grated Parmesan cheese

1 teaspoon salt

4 extra large eggs, room temperature

4 ounces (110 g) baby arugula

COOK

Vinaigrette

In a small bowl, whisk together the oil, mustard, vinegar, salt, and pepper; set aside.

Polenta

Pour 4 cups (960 ml) water and milk into the French oven; add the bouillon cubes, white pepper, cayenne pepper, and mustard. Bring to a boil over medium heat while whisking to dissolve the bouillon, reduce the heat, and then slowly sprinkle in handfuls of cornmeal as you whisk to combine. When all the cornmeal is in, keep stirring for about 2 minutes, until you see it start to thicken and make plopping sounds.

Reduce the heat to low and stir frequently as it cooks. After 8 minutes it should be very, very thick. Whisk in ½ cup (120 ml) water and keep cooking on low, so you will hear it almost hissing.

After 5 more minutes, add remaining water and stir until the polenta is looser and fluffy. Cook for 5 minutes more. Whisk in the butter and cheese then cover while you start cooking the eggs.

In a large skillet, heat an inch of water until it forms bubbles around the edges. Add 1 teaspoon salt and stir. Gently slip in the eggs, 1 at a time. Cover the skillet, turn off the heat, and let sit for 3 minutes. Uncover and gently touch an egg with your finger. If it is too soft for you, cover and let set 1 more minute. You want the poached eggs to be soft enough so that when they are pierced with a fork they run in rivulets down the polenta.

While the eggs are cooking, divide the hot polenta between 4 shallow bowls or plates (if it has thickened, add 1 to 2 tablespoons water and whisk until fluffy). Toss the arugula with enough of the vinaigrette to coat then divide on top of the polenta in each plate.

With a slotted spoon, transfer a poached egg to sit on the salad in each bowl. Serve. Have a pepper mill and sea salt nearby.

IDEAS AND SUGGESTIONS

Instead of Parmesan, whisk in 4 ounces (110 g) soft goat cheese.

CHICKEN BREASTS STUFFED WITH HAM, MUSHROOMS, AND CHEESE

Suprêmes de Poulet Farcis au Jambon, aux Champignons et au Fromage SERVES 6

I learned to make this dish when I lived in Paris in the early 1980s and it remains one of my go-to dishes for company on blustery cold days. I drizzle the sauce over wild rice, top it with a chicken breast, and pair it with a chilled dry white wine.

SPECIAL EQUIPMENT PASTRY BRUSH; 5-QUART (5-L) OR LARGER FRENCH OVEN; INSTANT-READ THERMOMETER

½ cup (120 ml) cognac or brandy, divided

6 boneless chicken breasts with skins

Salt and coarsely ground black pepper, to taste

3 tablespoons (45 g) butter, divided

8 ounces (225 g) button mushrooms, finely chopped

2 large cloves garlic, minced

1 teaspoon Dijon mustard

3 ounces (90 g) prosciutto, finely chopped

4 ounces (110 g) Gruyère cheese, grated, plus 6 thin slices

3 tablespoons (45 ml) extra virgin olive oil

1 teaspoon tomato paste

3 teaspoons all-purpose flour

1½ cups (360 ml) chicken stock

1 cup (240 ml) dry or medium dry Madeira wine

1 teaspoon sugar

6 tablespoons (40 g) freshly grated Parmesan cheese, divided

COOK

Pour 2 tablespoons (30 ml) cognac into a small bowl. Slice a pocket in each chicken breast, and with the pastry brush, coat the insides with the cognac. Sprinkle salt and pepper into the pockets. Let the breasts rest until ready to stuff.

Melt 2 tablespoons (30 g) butter in a large skillet, toss in the mushrooms and garlic and sprinkle in salt and coarsely ground black pepper. Cook over medium heat for 2 minutes. Remove from the heat; mix in the mustard, 1 tablespoon (15 ml) cognac, and the prosciutto. Transfer to a plate to cool to room temperature.

Mix the grated Gruyère into the mushroom mixture and use to stuff the chicken breasts.

In the French oven, heat oil over medium heat until shimmering hot then place each chicken breast, skin side down, into the hot oil, and brown on both sides.

In a small saucepan, heat remaining cognac. Turn off the heat. Ignite the cognac with a match and pour it over the chicken breasts. Transfer the breasts to a plate.

Melt remaining butter in the French oven, add the tomato paste and flour and stir over medium heat for 1 minute. Whisk in the stock, Madeira, sugar, and 4 cracks of black pepper and mix until smooth. Bring to a boil over medium heat then reduce to a low simmer. Place the chicken breasts in the sauce, cover, and cook on low heat until the chicken is cooked through, about 15–20 minutes, or when the thermometer reads 165° F (74° C).

Preheat the broiler.

Take the lid off the French oven, place a slice of Gruyère cheese on each chicken breast, sprinkle 1 tablespoon Parmesan cheese over the top of each, and place the French oven under the broiler until the cheese is melted and browned a little. Serve.

IDEAS AND SUGGESTIONS

You can substitute Swiss cheese for the Gruyère. Add finely chopped walnuts or sun-dried tomatoes to the stuffing or Gorgonzola and prunes. Add a splash of cream to the sauce before running under the broiler.

BASQUE-STYLE PAELLA

Paëlla à la Basque SERVES 6 TO 8

In French Basque cooking, red bell peppers, piment d'Espelette (the slightly smoky paprika from that region), and Bayonne ham are found in an endless variety of dishes. When making paella, I reach for these French Basque ingredients and combine them with chicken, shrimp, and mussels. Instead of the traditional addition of saffron, I use turmeric to color my rice to a sunny yellow worthy of creating a bed for the many colors of the paella that will nestle into it.

SPECIAL EQUIPMENT OVENPROOF SKILLET; 5-QUART (5-L) OR LARGER FRENCH OVEN

2 pounds (900 g) mussels

16 medium or large shrimp

2 cups (480 ml) water

6 tablespoons (90 ml) extra virgin olive oil, divided

1 cup (120 g) thinly sliced half moons chorizo sausage

8 boneless chicken thighs with skin

Salt and pepper, to taste

1 medium yellow onion, finely chopped

4 large cloves garlic

2 large red bell peppers, sliced into ¼-inch (.5-cm) strips

2 cups (400 g) short-grain rice or Arborio rice

6 to 7 cups (1.4 l to 1.7 l) chicken stock

1 tablespoon ground turmeric

2 teaspoons piment d'Espelette (smoked paprika, or sweet paprika as an alternative)

2 tablespoons fresh thyme leaves

½ teaspoon crushed red pepper flakes

1 (8-ounce / 227-g) jar roasted red peppers, sliced into thin strips

6 ounces (170 g) prosciutto (or French Jambon de Bayonne if you have access to it), sliced into ½-inch (1.5-cm) wide ribbons

2 organic lemons, quartered

¼ bunch flat-leaf parsley, stemmed and leaves minced

PREP

Preheat oven to 475° F (250° C). Wash the mussels under running water, scrubbing them well and pulling off their beards. Throw away any that are open. Peel and devein shrimp, leaving the tail on.

COOK

Put the mussels in the French oven with water, cover, and cook over medium heat until they open. Remove with a slotted spoon to a bowl. Save the cooking liquid in a measuring cup.

Wipe out the French oven, add 3 tablespoons (45 ml) oil, toss in the chorizo and cook over medium-low heat until the oil is well flavored from the chorizo, about 5 minutes. Remove the chorizo to a large bowl. Keep the oil in the French oven.

Liberally season the chicken with salt and pepper. In the ovenproof skillet, heat remaining oil until shimmering hot, add the chicken, and brown on all sides, 10–14 minutes. Transfer the skillet to the hot oven for another 17 minutes, or until the chicken is

cooked. Remove from the oven and toss the chicken into the bowl.

Add a little more oil to the skillet, if needed, heat until it is shimmering hot, toss in the shrimp, and cook on medium until pink. Transfer to the bowl.

Add a little more oil to the French oven, if needed, and when it is shimmering hot, toss in the onion, garlic, and bell peppers and cook on medium for 6 minutes.

Add the rice, stock, turmeric, piment d'Espelette, thyme, and crushed red pepper flakes. Bring to a boil over medium heat, reduce to a simmer, cover, and cook for about 20 minutes, until the rice is cooked.

Nestle the contents from the bowl into the rice in the French oven. Garnish with roasted red pepper and prosciutto. Add lemon quarters, sprinkle with parsley, and bring to the table to serve.

IDEAS AND SUGGESTIONS

Add frozen baby peas to the rice after it is cooked.

WHOLE STUFFED AND POACHED CHICKEN WITH APPLES AND CIDER SAUCE

Poulet Farci et Poché, Sauce à la Pomme et au Cidre SERVES 6

Poaching a whole chicken, a stuffed one, in a French oven with chicken stock and vegetables, including serving it with a creamy apple cider sauce, may seem a bit unusual, but it is perfectly normal in France where it is called poule au pot.

The components for the recipe vary from region to region, but at its core it is a stuffed chicken with vegetables and broth dish where the broth is served first as a soup. The chicken and stuffing and vegetables are then brought to the table as the next course.

Some recipes in the southwest of France use foie gras in the stuffing, but in the Normandy region it could easily be made using apples, ciders, and cream, and it is that combination that propelled me to create this recipe. I slice the chicken and scoop out the stuffing, arranging them on each plate, then ladle the sauce over the top. I save the poaching broth for soup later in the week.

SPECIAL EQUIPMENT 5-QUART (5-L) OR LARGER FRENCH OVEN; FOOD PROCESSOR; KITCHEN TWINE OR SKEWERS; MEAT THERMOMETER; ALUMINUM FOIL

1 (5- to 6-pound / 2. 3- to 2.7-kg) roasting chicken (measure to ensure it will fit in your French oven)

Stuffing

2 slices white bread

1/2 cup (120 ml) milk

2 tablespoons (30 ml) extra virgin olive oil

1 chicken liver (that came in chicken cavity) sliced into small pieces

1 boneless, skinless chicken breast, sliced

1/4 teaspoon salt

Freshly ground black pepper, to taste

2 shallots, sliced

4 large cloves garlic, sliced

4 sprigs parsley

1 (1/4-inch / .5-cm) thick slice ham, cut into cubes

2 large egg yolks

1 teaspoon kosher or sea salt

12 cracks coarsely ground black pepper

1/4 teaspoon ground nutmeg

1/2 cup (75 g) raisins

French Oven

2 cups (480 ml) water

2 chicken bouillon cubes

4 large cloves garlic, minced

4 sprigs parsley, leaves only, coarsely chopped

1 Granny Smith apple, peeled and finely chopped

1 chicken gizzard and neck (that came in chicken cavity)

1 medium carrot, grated

1 stalk celery with leaves, sliced and leaves chopped

Sauce

2 tablespoons (30 g) unsalted butter

1 Granny Smith apple, peeled and finely chopped

1/2 teaspoon sea salt

1/4 teaspoon ground sage

8 ounces (240 ml) fresh apple cider

3 tablespoons (25 g) all-purpose flour

3 tablespoons (45 g) half-and-half

Buttered egg noodles

PREP

Empty out the chicken cavity. Rinse the chicken and pat dry.

COOK

Stuffing

Soak bread in the milk then squeeze very dry. Discard milk.

In the French oven, heat the oil to shimmering hot over medium heat then toss in the liver, sliced chicken, salt, and pepper and cook to sear and slightly brown.

Remove the liver and chicken from the French oven and place into the food processor. Add the shallots, garlic, parsley, ham, egg yolks, bread, salt, pepper, and nutmeg and process for about 1 minute, until it is smooth. Stir in the raisins.

Stuff the chicken with this mixture and skewer, sew, or use twine to close up the chicken cavity. Place the chicken into the French oven.

French Oven

Add the water and bouillon cubes to a glass measuring cup and microwave for 1 minute. With a fork, mix well until cubes are dissolved and pour over the chicken in the French oven. Add garlic, parsley, and apple and tuck the gizzard and neck along the side. Add the carrot and sliced celery.

Cover, bring to a simmer, and then cook for 30 minutes, breast side up. Turn the chicken over, partially cover, and cook for another 30 minutes. When the chicken reaches 165°F (74° C) on the meat thermometer it is done. If not, simmer until it reaches this temperature.

Remove the chicken to a carving board or serving platter and loosely tent with aluminum foil until ready to carve.

Sauce

Melt the butter in a saucepan, add the apple, salt, and sage and cook until the apple is tender, about 4 minutes. Pour in the apple cider and 1 cup (240 ml) of stock from the French oven and heat to a simmer.

Combine the flour and enough water in a cup to make a thin batter. Slowly whisk into the cider sauce, bring back to a simmer, and whisk until thickened. Whisk in the half-and-half and taste, adding salt and pepper, if desired. Heat to a simmer and pour into a gravy boat.

Carve the chicken, arrange on each plate, spoon out some of the stuffing to the side, and serve with the sauce. Pour some of the stock from the French oven over the buttered noodles and serve them in a bowl.

IDEAS AND SUGGESTIONS

Use prosciutto in the stuffing. Use half stock and half white wine to poach the chicken.

NOS SPECIALITÉS

Les Poissons

Pot au Feu de la Mer
Brochette de St Jacques
Méli - Mélo de la Mer
Filet de St Pierre
Assiette de la Mer

ROASTING

Rather than roasting in metallic pans, a roast, in my mind, should be cooked in a French oven, where it will develop a crisper skin or crust from the closeness of the interior walls emanating heat evenly around the roast, helping it brown on all sides. Shallow roasting pans cannot do this.

Cook your roasts on a bed of vegetables so they receive all the rendered-fat goodness from the cooking roast above, while providing an instant side dish. Whether it is a roasted duck sitting on thickly cut potatoes, or chicken or beef or lamb on root vegetables, the resulting meal of juicy meat, crispy skin, and lusciously flavored soft vegetables will come to define what a great home-cooked meal is all about.

For me, there's nothing better than bringing a Sunday roast to the table in a beautiful French oven and carving and serving it there.

SIMPLY DELICIOUS ROASTED VEGETABLES

Légumes Rôtis juste Délicieux SERVES 4

Roasting a tangle of mixed vegetables in a French oven yields the most succulent and satisfying way to cook them, bringing out their flavors and producing great texture. I serve this at Thanksgiving and double the recipe if I have guests who prefer vegetables to turkey. It has a tiny hint of sweetness from the honey, and the vegetables are caramelized and tender. I either serve them from the French oven or stuff them into individual mini cocottes.

SPECIAL EQUIPMENT 5.5-QUART (5.5-L) OR LARGER FRENCH OVEN

3 medium parsnips

1 medium sweet potato

4 medium carrots

1 medium red onion

¼ cup (60 ml) extra virgin olive oil, plus 1 tablespoon (15 ml)

1 tablespoon (15 g) honey

2 teaspoons red wine vinegar

½ teaspoon ground cinnamon

½ teaspoon crushed red pepper flakes

½ teaspoon dried thyme

1 teaspoon salt

6 cracks coarsely ground black pepper

1 pound (450 g) mixed tiny potatoes or fingerlings

8 large cloves garlic

1 cup (150 g) raisins

PREP

Preheat oven to 450° F (230° C).

Slice off the root ends of the parsnips. Peel parsnips, slice into 4-inch (10-cm) pieces then slice them lengthwise into 4 spears if they are thin, or 6 spears if they are thick. Toss into a large bowl.

Peel sweet potato. Slice lengthwise into 4-inch (10-cm) pieces, or in half then slice into 6 spears. Toss in the bowl.

Slice the carrots lengthwise in half and again lengthwise in half. Toss in the bowl.

Peel onion. Slice into quarters then slice quarters into halves. Pull them apart into petals. Reserve.

COOK

Whisk together ¼ cup (60 ml) oil, honey, vinegar, cinnamon, red pepper flakes, thyme, salt, and pepper. Pour 3 tablespoons (45 ml) of this mixture into the bowl, add the potatoes, and toss everything with your hands to thoroughly coat.

Add remaining oil to the French oven, pour in the contents of the bowl, put into the oven, uncovered, and roast for 15 minutes. Stir. Reduce the heat to 375° F (190° C) and roast for another 25 minutes.

Toss the onion, garlic, and raisins into the bowl, pour in the remaining oil mixture and toss with a fork to coat. Pour it all into to the French oven and toss everything together with a fork.

Return to the oven and roast for another 25 minutes. Remove from the oven and serve either in the French oven or in individual mini cocottes.

IDEAS AND SUGGESTIONS

As a garnish, grate orange zest over the top.

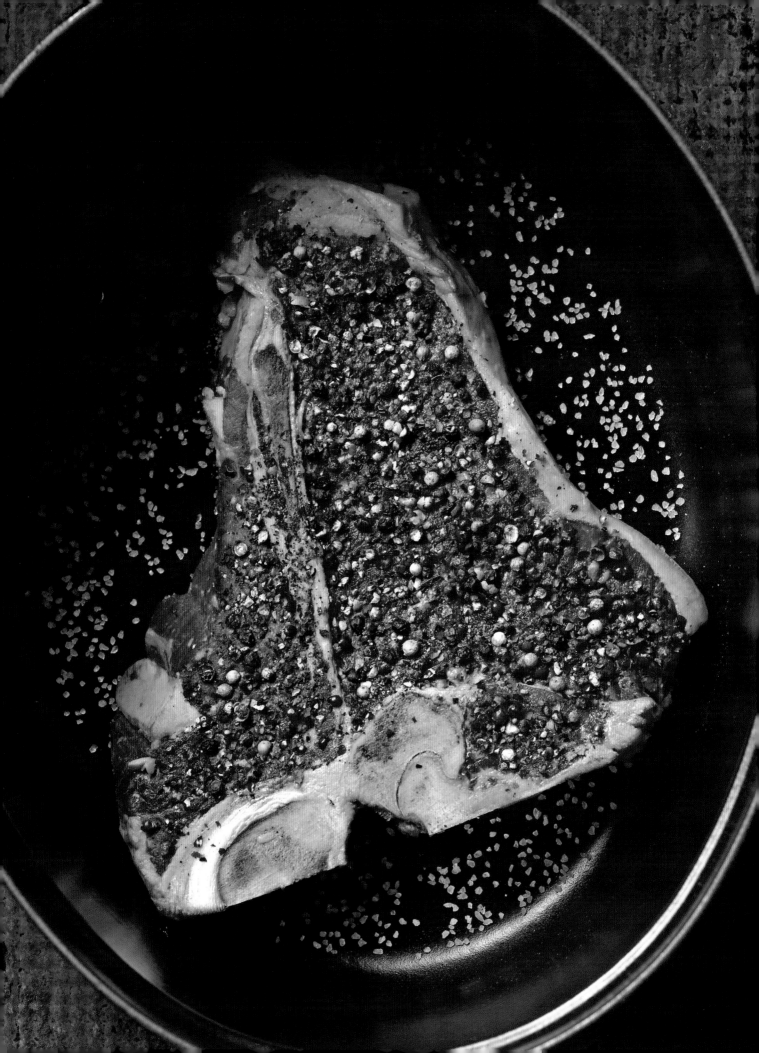

QUICK ROASTED STEAK AU POIVRE

Steak au Poivre Vite Rôti SERVES 4

After my grandmother cooked a porterhouse steak for us, she would lay it on a carving board over slices of bread while it rested. Then she would slice it right on the bread below. The juices would seep down as she carved each slice and transferred it to our waiting plates, and we would break out in smiles when she portioned out a bit of the juice-soaked bread to each plate. I continue this tradition in my own home today, except when I make it for company, and I encourage you to try it with this recipe.

This is a steak au poivre recipe using a porterhouse steak, one of my favorite cuts of meat. Buy the best quality steak you can as this is the star of the meal.

The recipe goes so quickly that you should make anything you are serving with it first. Salad should be in the bowl and dressed. Mashed potatoes should be under a loose tent of aluminum foil keeping warm.

SPECIAL EQUIPMENT MORTAR AND PESTLE; 5- TO 6-QUART (5- TO 6-L) FRENCH OVEN; MEAT THERMOMETER

2½ tablespoons (20 g) whole mixed peppercorns (black, white, and pink)

1 (1½- to 2-pound/ 700- to 900-g) porterhouse steak, 1½ inches (4 cm) thick or thicker, room temperature for 1 hour

3 tablespoons (45 ml) olive oil, divided

2 teaspoons kosher or sea salt

2 tablespoons (30 g) unsalted butter

1 large shallot, peeled and minced

1 beef bouillon cube

2 teaspoons (15 g) cornstarch

1 cup (240 g) heavy cream, room temperature

¼ cup (60 ml) cognac or brandy, optional but traditional

PREP

Preheat oven to 450° F (230° C).

Coarsely crack the peppercorns in the mortar and pestle or put them in a plastic bag and hit them with the back of a heavy knife or rolling pin to crush.

Rinse the steak then pat very dry with paper towels. Rub all over with 1 tablespoon oil. Season each side with 1 teaspoon salt. Spread 2¼ tablespoons (18 g) crushed peppercorns over the top of the steak and firmly press down with your fingers so that they adhere to the steak. Only do this to one side.

COOK

Add remaining oil to the French oven, place over medium heat, and when it is shimmering hot, add the steak, peppercorn side up. Sear the underside until golden brown, without moving, for about 1 minute.

Place the French oven in the oven to roast the steak. How long depends on the thickness and size of your steak, so instead of minutes, go by your meat thermometer inserted into the thickest part of the meat. Start checking the thermometer after 7 minutes of cooking. When it reads 120° to 125° F (50° to 52° C) it is rare, 130° to 135° F (55° to 57° C) medium rare, 135° to 140° F (57° to 60 °C) medium, and 160° to 170° F (71° to 77° C) well done.

Transfer the steak to a carving board to rest for 20 minutes.

Meanwhile, make the sauce. Put the French oven on the stove and melt butter over low heat. Stir in the shallot and remaining cracked peppercorns. Scrape

continued >

in the bouillon cube and then cook over medium heat for 3 minutes.

Mix the cornstarch with enough water to make a thin paste then whisk into the butter mixture. Pour in the cream and cognac, raise the heat to medium, and keep whisking until the sauce is thickened and well blended. Taste for seasoning and add more salt or coarsely ground black pepper, if desired. If the cognac flavor is too strong for you, cook the sauce a few minutes longer or add a little more cream or milk to the sauce until it pleases your palate.

To serve, slice off the smaller tenderloin and the bigger top loin piece away from the steak bone. Slice these pieces and divide between plates, giving each plate a little of each.

Drizzle the sauce over the slices of steak. Serve with kosher or sea salt and a pepper grinder on the table, as well as any sides you prepared before cooking the steak.

IDEAS AND SUGGESTIONS

Instead, make a simple wine sauce for the steak. Put 3 tablespoons (25 g) minced shallots and 1 cup (240 ml) red wine in a saucepan. Simmer until reduced by half, whisk in 4 tablespoons (60 g) butter until melted and combined, then drizzle over steak.

AN ELEGANT STANDING BEEF RIB ROAST

Un Élégant Train de Côtes de Boeuf SERVES 4

Taking a spoonful of the vegetables into my mouth, I could taste the fat and the seasonings that had drizzled down to coat them as the roast cooked. Luscious! I decided then and there it was the only way to roast.

My French oven, plus the way the vegetables and meat were arranged, had made the difference. The high sides of the French oven evenly roasted the gorgeous beef rib roast, while the vegetables below held it in place, receiving all the juices from the cooking meat.

This is a magnificent dish to serve company. One 2-bone-in rib roast will easily serve 4.

SPECIAL EQUIPMENT 5-QUART (5-L) OR LARGER FRENCH OVEN; INSTANT-READ MEAT THERMOMETER; ALUMINUM FOIL

1 (5-pound / 2.3-kg) 2-bone-in standing rib roast, room temperature

Olive oil for exterior of roast, plus 3 tablespoons (45 ml)

Salt and freshly ground pepper, to taste

3 russet potatoes

4 carrots, peeled and sliced into 2-inch (5-cm) pieces

2 stalks celery, sliced into 2-inch (5-cm) pieces

8 large cloves garlic

½ teaspoon salt

4 cracks coarsely ground black pepper

PREP

Preheat oven to 450° F (230° C).

Pat dry the roast with paper towels. Rub with a little olive oil then season all over with salt and freshly ground pepper.

Wash and dry potatoes. Slice each vertically then cut into quarters. Place in a bowl of water until ready to use.

COOK

Pour 3 tablespoons (45 ml) oil into bottom of the French oven. Toss in the potatoes, carrots, celery, and garlic with skins on. Sprinkle with the salt and coarsely ground black pepper.

Using the vegetables as a bed, place the roast, fat side down, on top of the vegetables.

Place in the oven and cook for 15 minutes. Reduce the heat to 365° F (185° C), and cook for 1 hour and 10 minutes.

Turn the roast over. Return to oven and cook another half hour.

Insert the thermometer into the thickest part of the roast. If you would like it rare, it should read between 110° and 115° F (between 43° and 46° C). For medium rare, take it out when it reads 125° to 130° F (52° to 55° C). For medium, take it out when it reads 135° to 140° F (57° C to 60° C). For well done, take it out when it reads 160° F (71° C).

Transfer the roast to a carving board and let rest for 15 minutes with a piece of aluminum foil tented over it. Put the cover on the French oven to keep the vegetables warm.

To carve, lay the rib roast on its side and make slices parallel to the bone from the outer edge inwards. Then slice the meat away from the bones, and slice as thin or thick as you like.

IDEAS AND SUGGESTIONS

Serve with a chilled horseradish sauce: blend 2 ounces (60 g) bottled horseradish, zest from 1 lemon, 2 cups (480 g) sour cream, 1 teaspoon Dijon mustard, and lots of minced chives.

ROAST TURKEY BREAST WITH PROVENÇAL VEGETABLES

Rôti de Dinde et Légumes à la Provençale SERVES 6 TO 8

As an alternative when you don't want to cook a whole turkey, this recipe for roasting a turkey breast takes significantly less time and yields a great tasting meal, complete with vegetables.

Remember to make sure to carry a measuring tape with you when you buy your turkey breast so that it just fits into your French oven, or have the butcher measure it for you.

SPECIAL EQUIPMENT 5-QUART (5-L) OR LARGER FRENCH OVEN; INSTANT-READ MEAT THERMOMETER; ALUMINUM FOIL

1 (4- to 5-pound / 1.8- to 2.3-kg) boneless turkey breast with skin or 2 (2- to 2½-pound / 900- to 1.2-kg) boneless turkey breast halves with skin

11 tablespoons (165 ml) extra virgin olive oil, divided

2 teaspoons salt, divided

2 teaspoons garlic powder, divided

4 tablespoons herbes de Provence, divided

2 russet potatoes

2 small sweet potatoes

2 medium onions, sliced into ½-inch (1.5-cm) wedges

1 stalk celery, sliced into 2-inch (5-cm) pieces

8 large cloves garlic

3 cups (720 ml) chicken or turkey stock

1 tablespoon cornstarch, plus more, if needed

Salt and pepper, to taste

½ (14-ounce / 397-g) can whole cranberries, optional

PREP

If your turkey breast is frozen, completely thaw it according to package instructions.

Preheat oven to 450° F (230° C). Put rack in the middle of the oven to allow for the height of the French oven with the turkey breast.

In a small bowl, mix 4 tablespoons (60 ml) oil, 1 teaspoon salt, 1 teaspoon garlic powder, and 2 tablespoons herbes de Provence together. Repeat this process in another small bowl.

Slice potatoes vertically then into ¼-inch (½-cm) slices. Place in a bowl of water until ready to use.

COOK

Wash and pat dry the turkey breast. Insert your fingers under the skin and massage in olive oil mixture from one of the small bowls under the skin then all over the roast. Pour remaining oil from the bowl into bottom of French oven.

Drain the potatoes and pat very dry. Dry the bowl. Put the potatoes back into the bowl. Add the onions, celery, and garlic. Pour in the olive oil mixture from the second small bowl and toss the vegetables to completely coat. Pour everything into the bottom of the French oven. Using the vegetables as a bed, place the turkey, fat side down, on top of the vegetables.

If you are cooking the whole turkey breast, cook it for 45–60 minutes, basting several times, then test with the meat thermometer in the thickest part of the breast. It should read 155° to 160° F (68° to 71° C). If not there yet, baste and then roast for another 20 minutes before checking the temperature again. Remove turkey from the oven and transfer to a carving board. Loosely tent with aluminum foil and let rest for 20 minutes.

If you are cooking the turkey halves, place in the oven, reduce heat to 375° F (190° C) and cook for 30 minutes. Baste the turkey then reduce heat to 325° F (165° C) and roast for 20 minutes. Turn the turkey breasts over, baste, and then roast another 15 minutes. Check with the meat thermometer in the thickest part of the breast. If it registers 155° to 160° F (66° to 71° C), remove from oven, cover loosely with foil, and let rest for 20 minutes. The internal temperature will rise to 170° F (77° C).

With a slotted spoon, transfer the vegetables, leaving the garlic, to a serving bowl and loosely tent with aluminum foil.

Move the French oven to the stovetop over medium heat. Mash the garlic cloves with a fork.

Pour in the stock and bring to a simmer. Sprinkle in the cornstarch and vigorously whisk until the gravy thickens and the browned bits come up from the bottom. If you would like the gravy thicker, add another tablespoon of cornstarch and whisk until the gravy thickens more. Season with salt and pepper. If you would like a fruity gravy, spoon in half or more of the can of cranberries and whisk well.

Place some vegetables on each plate. Thinly slice the turkey. Fan slices of turkey around them. Ladle over the gravy and serve.

IDEAS AND SUGGESTIONS

Serve with cranberry sauce. Even if it isn't Thanksgiving, it rounds out the flavors in this recipe in a wonderful way.

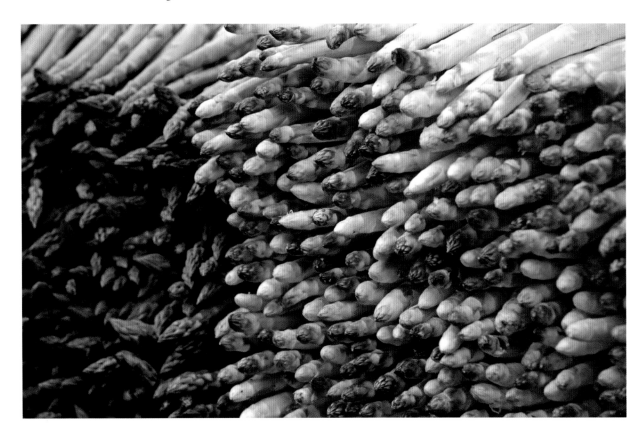

SPICY CHICKEN À LA DIABLE WITH MUSTARD SAUCE

Poulet Épicé à la Diable, Sauce à la Moutarde SERVES 4

Poulet à la diable *refers to a way of cooking chicken where it is cut into pieces, sprinkled with breadcrumbs mixed with mustard and cayenne, and broiled or grilled—then served with a* diable *sauce, made with a roux, white wine, herbs, and cayenne.*

I have taken the idea of a diable sauce and played with it a bit, adding mustard and cream and tarragon and some diced fresh tomatoes to brighten it up. The combination of the hot spicy chicken with the sauce was so addictive the first time I made it, that I made it most of that summer, sometimes grilling the chicken on the barbecue, sometimes roasting it in a French oven.

SPECIAL EQUIPMENT 5-QUART (5-L) OR LARGER FRENCH OVEN; PASTRY BRUSH; INSTANT-READ THERMOMETER

- 1 (4- to 5-pound / 1.8- to 2.3-kg) chicken to fit your French oven
- 2 sprigs fresh tarragon or 2 teaspoons dried tarragon
- 2 tablespoons (30 ml) extra virgin olive oil, plus extra to rub on chicken
- 2 medium russet potatoes, peeled and sliced into ¼-inch (.5-cm) matchsticks
- Salt and coarsely ground black pepper, to taste

- 3 tablespoons (45 g) stone-ground mustard
- ¼ teaspoon cayenne pepper
- 1 teaspoon honey or sugar
- 1 teaspoon dried thyme
- ½ cup (45 g) seasoned breadcrumbs
- 2 tablespoons (15 g) minced shallot (1 medium to large shallot)
- ¼ cup (60 ml) white wine vinegar

- ¼ cup (60 ml) dry white wine
- 1½ cups (360 ml) chicken stock
- 2 large cloves garlic, minced
- ½ teaspoon salt
- ½ teaspoon Dijon mustard
- ⅛ teaspoon cayenne
- ½ cup (120 g) heavy cream
- 1 medium tomato, cut into small dice with seeds and juice reserved

PREP

Preheat oven to 400° F (200° C). Rinse and pat chicken very dry. Pull tarragon leaves off stems, discard stems, and finely chop leaves.

COOK

Pour oil into the French oven. Toss in the potato matchsticks and season with salt and pepper. If there is a giblet or liver in the cavity of the chicken, take it out and toss it in with the potatoes, to add flavor.

Place the chicken on the bed of potatoes. Rub it all over with olive oil then liberally season with salt and pepper. Place the French oven in the oven to roast for 15 minutes per pound. A 4-pound (1.8-kg) chicken should roast for 45 minutes. A 5-pound (2.3-kg) chicken should roast for 1 hour.

Meanwhile, whisk together the mustard, cayenne, honey, and thyme. Set aside.

When the chicken is ready, take the French oven out of the oven and apply the mustard mixture all over the chicken with the pastry brush. Shake the breadcrumbs all over the mustard, pat down gently

so they adhere, then return the chicken to the oven to roast for an additional 15–20 minutes, until the breadcrumbs are golden and crispy. The chicken should read 165° F (74° C) on the thermometer. Take it out of the oven and transfer the chicken to a carving board. Transfer the potatoes to a large plate or serving bowl.

Place the French oven on the stovetop. Add the shallot, vinegar, wine, and half of tarragon and bring to a simmer. Cook for 5 minutes. Add the stock, garlic, ½ teaspoon salt, mustard, cayenne, and cream and simmer for 10 minutes. Just before serving, stir in the remaining tarragon and the tomato and its seeds and juice. Stir and cook an additional 2 minutes.

Ladle sauce on one side of each plate. Top with slices of chicken and a scoop of the potatoes on the side.

IDEAS AND SUGGESTIONS

Eliminate the mustard mixture if you would like a less spicy version.

TWO HANDS PRAYING RACK OF LAMB ROAST

Trains de Côtes d'Agneau Grillées, comme Deux Mains qui Prient SERVES 4 TO 6

When I entwined the bones from two racks of lamb, fitting them in between each other, as if two hands were praying, it resulted in my naming this recipe. You can easily do it yourself or have the butcher prepare two identical racks of lamb and entwine them for you. Measure your French oven to decide how long each rack should be to fit into it.

It makes a simply elegant meal for a special occasion dinner, one where you want to use your best china and bring out that expensive wine you have been saving.

SPECIAL EQUIPMENT 5-QUART (5-L) OR LARGER FRENCH OVEN; FOOD PROCESSOR; MEAT THERMOMETER

- 1½ pounds (700 g) russet potatoes, peeled and cut into ¼-inch (.5-cm) pieces
- 1 pound (450 g) turnips, peeled and cut into ¼-inch (.5-cm) pieces
- 2 (6-rib) racks of lamb
- 3 tablespoons (45 ml) extra virgin olive oil, plus ¼ cup (60 ml)
- 6 large shallots, thickly sliced

- 16 large cloves garlic, divided
- 2 medium carrots, cut into ¼-inch (.5-cm) pieces
- 2 tablespoons (30 g) finely chopped fresh rosemary, divided
- 2 teaspoons kosher or sea salt or salt flakes, divided
- 10 cracks coarsely ground black pepper, divided

- ½ pound (225 g) bunch red or green grapes, in small clusters on stems
- 1 tablespoon (15 g) unsalted butter, softened
- 1 tablespoon (15 g) chutney
- 1 cup (240 ml) dry sherry
- 2 tablespoons (30 g) currant jelly

PREP

Preheat oven to 450° F (230° C). Place cut potatoes and turnips into a bowl of cold water until ready to use. Rinse and pat very dry the racks of lamb with paper towels.

COOK

Pour 3 tablespoons (45 ml) oil into the French oven. Drain and pat the potatoes and turnips very dry with paper towels then add to the French oven. Toss in the shallots, 12 whole cloves garlic, carrots, 1 tablespoon (15 g) rosemary, 1 teaspoon salt, and 6 cracks pepper. Over medium heat, sauté the vegetables for 20 minutes.

Toss remaining garlic, rosemary, oil, salt, and pepper into the food processor and process until smooth to make a rub.

Place the racks of lamb together, entwining the ribs as if they were hands praying, and place them onto the bed of vegetables in the French oven. Tuck the grape clusters around the sides of the roast.

Rub the roast with the contents from the food processor. Roast in the oven for 30–40 minutes. When the lamb reaches 130° F (55° C) on the meat thermometer, it will be medium rare; 135° to 140° F (57° to 60° C) for medium; 145° to 150° F (63° to 66° C) for well done.

Take out of the oven and let rest for 10 minutes before bringing to the table or putting it on the carving board to slice.

Melt the butter in a saucepan. Add chutney, sherry, and jelly and bring to a boil. Whisk for 1 minute to combine.

Slice the roast and place lamb on each plate with a serving of the vegetables to the side. Drizzle the sauce over the lamb and serve.

IDEAS AND SUGGESTIONS

Make a tapenade rub for the lamb instead. Process in a food processor, 8 pitted oil-cured black olives, 1/2 teaspoon capers, 1 large clove garlic, 1 teaspoon anchovy paste or 2 anchovy filets, and drizzle in up to 1/4 cup (60 ml) extra virgin olive oil to make a paste. Some of this will trickle down to the cooking vegetables below the roast adding flavor as they cook.

BRAISING

Long braising is a technique of cooking that works well with inexpensive and tougher cuts of meat. Think slow when you braise in a French oven, because it is ideal for slowly conducting heat. However, short braising works more quickly and equally well with delicate ingredients like fish or vegetables, yielding the same succulent texture and intensely flavored broth.

For both long and short braising, a tightly fitted lid is essential. Some French oven manufacturers make them with spikes so that when moisture rises from the food below, it hits the lid then is recycled by the spikes to drip like rain back down onto the food, self-basting without the need of you taking off the lid and basting yourself. And the process is constant and consistent.

Long braising means you first brown meats and poultry in the French oven on top of the stove, add in vegetables and aromatics, then add the liquid of your choice so that it reaches only halfway up the meat or poultry, cover with the lid, and cook in the oven or on the stove at a low temperature for a long time. The following recipes give you examples of both long and short methods.

BRAISED LEEKS AND SWISS CHARD WITH FETA AND RAISINS

Poireaux et Blettes Braisés, Feta et Raisins Secs SERVES 4

Short-braised vegetables are one of the unsung delights of cooking and one of my favorite dishes to make in a French oven. This one celebrates the flavors of the area around Nice where I lived. The Niçois love Swiss chard and put it in almost everything, so it is the star in this braised mix of rainbow colored chard and leeks, with some anchovies, raisins, orange, and feta to layer in intriguing flavors that filter down to create an intoxicatingly delicious broth that you can sop up with a toasted baguette.

SPECIAL EQUIPMENT 5-QUART (5-L) OR LARGER FRENCH OVEN

3 medium leeks

2 bunches Swiss chard (2 pounds / 900 g), rainbow or red if you can find it

3 tablespoons (45 ml) extra virgin olive oil, plus extra for drizzling

4 large cloves garlic, finely chopped

6 anchovy filets, coarsely chopped

3 tablespoons (45 g) raisins

Salt and coarsely ground black pepper, to taste

Freshly grated nutmeg

Pinch of crushed red pepper

¾ cup (180 ml) chicken stock

½ organic lemon, juiced

8 ounces (225 g) feta cheese

1 small organic orange, zested

PREP

Heat oven to 350° F (180° C).

Split leeks in half vertically then wash under running water. Pat dry with paper towels. Slice off the root end and 2 inches from the tops and discard. Pull off the tough outer layer and discard. Slice leek into ½-inch (1.5-cm) pieces.

Wash Swiss chard and pat dry. Slice off the root end. Slice the leaves from the stalk and slice the leaves into 1-inch (2.5-cm) pieces. Slice the stalks into ½-inch (1.5-cm) pieces.

COOK

Heat oil in the French oven over medium heat then add the garlic, anchovies, and raisins and cook for 2 minutes.

Toss in the leeks and Swiss chard stems. Generously season with salt, pepper, nutmeg, and crushed red pepper and stir everything to coat. Add the stock and lemon juice, bring to a boil, cover, and then place in the oven to braise for 25 minutes.

Add the Swiss chard leaves, stir, crumble the feta over the top, and braise, uncovered, in the oven for another 20 minutes. The feta will not melt but will be a warm soft layer on top.

Garnish with orange zest, drizzle with olive oil, and serve with toasted baguette.

IDEAS AND SUGGESTIONS

This is lovely tossed into warm pasta.

FORK-TENDER WINE-BRAISED SHORT RIBS

Plat-de-Côtes Fondant Braisé au Vin Rouge SERVES 4

Long marinating and long braising used together in this recipe produces an amazingly tender beef dish that is flavored with wine and herbes de Provence and served over wide noodles or mashed potatoes.

This is a long, slow cooking recipe perfect for a Sunday afternoon. It takes about 3 hours. When it is ready, light the fire, pour a glass of wine, and savor this very special dinner.

SPECIAL EQUIPMENT 5-QUART (5-L) OR LARGER FRENCH OVEN; ALUMINUM FOIL

1 bottle dry red wine (Cabernet Sauvignon, Shiraz, Merlot), divided

¼ teaspoon ground cloves

6 large cloves garlic, coarsely chopped, divided

1 bay leaf

2 large shallots, finely chopped

1 tablespoon herbes de Provence

1 teaspoon salt

8 (2- to 4-inch / 5- to 10-cm) beef bone-in short ribs, about 4 pounds (1.8 kg)

Salt and pepper to season ribs, plus more

2 tablespoons (15 g) all-purpose flour, plus more to dredge ribs

6 tablespoons (90 ml) extra virgin olive oil, divided, plus more if needed

1 medium onion, finely chopped

6 medium carrots, 2 diced and 4 cut into ½-inch (1.5-cm) pieces

2 stalks celery with leaves, finely chopped, reserve the leaves

1 beef bouillon cube

2 tablespoons (25 g) brown sugar

2 sprigs fresh sprigs thyme, leaves removed from stems, divided

2 sprigs fresh rosemary, leaves removed from stems and minced

2 tablespoons (30 g) unsalted butter

Boiled or mashed potatoes or cooked egg noodles

PREP

The day before you want to prepare the recipe, or the morning of the day you want to cook it, pour 2 cups (480 ml) wine into a large bowl. Add ground cloves, half the garlic, bay leaf, shallots, herbes de Provence, and salt. Whisk well to combine. Add the meat, turn to coat, cover with plastic wrap, and refrigerate until ready to use.

When you are ready to prepare the dish, remove the meat and marinade from the refrigerator. Transfer the meat to paper towels and pat very dry. Strain the marinade, discard the contents of the strainer, and reserve the liquid marinade for later. Liberally salt and pepper the meat, dredge it in flour, and shake off excess.

Preheat oven to 350° F (180° C).

COOK

Heat 3 tablespoons (45 ml) oil in the French oven over medium heat until shimmering hot, add half the ribs and brown on all sides, for about 3 minutes per side. Remove to a plate. Repeat with remaining short ribs. Wipe out the French oven with paper towels.

Add 3 tablespoons (45 ml) oil to the French oven, heat over medium heat until shimmering hot, and then add the onion, diced carrots, and celery and cook for 7 minutes, stirring frequently. Add the reserved marinade and crumble in the bouillon cube. Then add the ribs, salt, pepper, and the remaining garlic. At this point, judge if the liquid comes halfway up the sides of the meat. If not, add more wine then reserve the rest for later. The liquid will rise as steam and drip back down to baste the meat, so you only need it to reach halfway up the meat.

Bring to a boil over medium heat then reduce to a simmer. Put the lid on and place in the oven to braise for 2½ hours, turning the ribs a couple of times during cooking.

Blend 2 tablespoons (15 g) flour with ½ cup (120 ml) of the cooking liquid and whisk back into the French oven to make a sauce. Add the remaining carrots, brown sugar, half the thyme, and the rosemary. Stir, return to the oven without the lid, and cook for another 30 minutes, until the meat is fork tender.

To test, take a fork and twist the meat. If it comes off the bone easily, it is done. Cooking time will depend on the size and thickness of the ribs. Taste for seasoning and add more salt and pepper, if desired.

Take the meat out of the French oven and loosely cover with aluminum foil to keep warm.

Simmer the sauce over medium heat for 5 minutes or a bit longer to further thicken it. Taste, adjust seasoning, and add more of the reserved wine, if desired, for flavor. Whisk in the butter until it is completely melted.

Stack 2 ribs and vegetables on each plate along with potatoes or noodles, spoon sauce over the top, and garnish with remaining thyme leaves and the chopped celery leaves.

IDEAS AND SUGGESTIONS

If you have leftovers, serve it over creamy polenta or fettuccine the next day.

BEER-BRAISED BEEF BRISKET

Poitrine de Boeuf braisée à la Bière Brune SERVES 6

You can assemble this long-braising recipe ahead of time then put it in the oven during the day so it is ready for dinner. The total cooking time could take between 3–4 hours, depending on the thickness of your meat, resulting in meltingly tender slices of brisket and a lovely clear sauce.

The beauty of this dish, for me, is that because brisket is tough and takes a long time to cook, it gives me lots of time to do something else until it is done. It basically takes care of itself.

SPECIAL EQUIPMENT FRENCH OVEN THAT IS LARGE ENOUGH TO HOLD YOUR BRISKET; MEAT THERMOMETER

Salt and pepper, to taste

1 (3½- to 4-pound / 1.6- to 1.8-kg) beef brisket, trimmed of fat

4 tablespoons (60 ml) extra virgin olive oil

2 medium yellow onions, thinly sliced

3 tablespoons (35 g) dark brown sugar

1 beef bouillon cube

1 cup (240 ml) water

4 large cloves garlic, pressed or minced

3 sprigs fresh thyme, leaves removed and divided

3 bay leaves

½ teaspoon ground allspice

1 (12-ounce / 350-ml) can dark beer, stout, or porter

3 stalks celery with leaves, celery sliced and leaves chopped and divided

8 cracks coarsely ground black pepper

Cooked buttered noodles

PREP

Preheat oven to 325° F (160° C) and salt and pepper the brisket on both sides.

TO COOK

In the French oven, heat the oil and add the onions. Cook over medium heat until they begin to turn brown, about 15 minutes. Add brown sugar and continue to stir for another 3 minutes, or until the onions start to caramelize.

Melt the bouillon cube in the water in a microwave for 80 seconds then pour into the French oven over the onions.

Add the garlic, half of the thyme, bay leaves, allspice, beer, celery and two-thirds of leaves, and pepper to the French oven and stir to combine. Lay the brisket over the sauce. If the liquid does not come halfway up sides of brisket, add water. Place in the oven and bake for 1 hour, uncovered.

Turn the meat over, cover, and cook 1 hour. Turn the meat again, cover, and cook for another hour, or longer, until the meat is fork tender and the meat thermometer reads 155° F (68° C).

Remove the meat to a cutting board and let rest for 20 minutes. Slice against the grain and serve over buttered noodles. Ladle sauce over the meat and garnish with the remaining thyme and chopped celery leaves.

IDEAS AND SUGGESTIONS

Any leftovers make great sandwiches on crusty rolls.

BRAISED COD WITH POTATOES AND ONIONS

Cabillaud Braisé, Pommes de Terre et Oignons SERVES 4

Fresh cod is one of France's favorite fishes. Cabillaud or morue is prepared in all manner of ways, primarily with potatoes as the next most important ingredient. Cabillaud Parmentier, cod with a mashed potato crust, is ubiquitous in the freezer section of most supermarkets and on many restaurant menus.

Short-braising it, however, yields an unusually tender piece of fish and is my preferred way of preparing fresh cod. I created this recipe for the French oven with an underlying potato and onion base moistened with clam juice and cream. The pieces of cod are quickly braised over the top.

SPECIAL EQUIPMENT 5-QUART (5-L) OR LARGER FRENCH OVEN

Salt and coarsely ground pepper, to taste

4 (6-ounce / 170-g) filets cod

3 large cloves garlic, 2 finely chopped and 1 sliced in half

Olive oil

2 cups (480 ml) bottled clam juice

1 tablespoon fresh thyme or 1 teaspoon dried thyme

½ teaspoon salt

⅛ teaspoon cayenne pepper

¼ teaspoon paprika, plus ⅛ teaspoon (smoked or sweet)

1 bay leaf

2 medium yellow onions, thinly sliced

4 tablespoons (60 g) unsalted butter, 2 tablespoons (30 g) quartered

4 medium russet potatoes, peeled and cut into ⅛-inch (.5-cm) slices

½ cup (120 g) heavy cream

1 medium tomato, sliced into fine dice, saving the seeds and juice

½ organic lemon, zested and juiced

2 tablespoons finely chopped flat-leaf parsley

PREP

Preheat oven to 450° F (230° C) and salt and pepper both sides of the cod. Rub the insides of the French oven with the half cloves of garlic then rub on a thin film of olive oil.

COOK

Pour the clam juice into a saucepan. Add all of the garlic, including the half cloves, thyme, salt, cayenne, ¼ teaspoon paprika, and bay leaf. Bring to a boil over medium heat, reduce to a simmer, and cook for 5 minutes.

Meanwhile, arrange a layer of onions in the bottom of the French oven. Dot with 4 of the pieces of butter. Sprinkle salt and coarsely ground pepper over the top.

Arrange a layer of potatoes over the top of the onions. Dot with 4 of the pieces of butter. Season with salt and coarsely ground pepper. Keep alternating onions and potatoes until they are used up.

Discard the bay leaf that is in the clam juice. Pour the clam juice mixture over the top of the potatoes. Put the French oven on the stove and, over medium heat, bring the liquid to a simmer. Cover and place in the oven for 25 minutes.

Pour the cream into the saucepan that held the clam juice and bring to a simmer. Take the cover off the French oven, add the hot cream, then the tomato with its seeds and juice, and add the cod on top.

Mash 2 tablespoons (30 g) butter with the lemon zest and juice and remaining paprika. Divide into fourths and place a portion on top of each filet of cod. Cover and return to the oven to braise for 12–15 minutes, depending on the thickness of the fish, until the cod is flaky and cooked through. Garnish with minced parsley and serve.

IDEAS AND SUGGESTIONS

Add another layer of flavor consisting of finely shaved fennel, celery, and finely sliced leeks.

LEMON-BRAISED CHICKEN WITH GREEN OLIVES

Poulet Braisé au Citron et aux Olives Vertes SERVES 4

Lots of delicious gravy for ladling over buttered noodles is one of the best parts of this slow-braising recipe for chicken. There are a host of vibrant tastes going on in this dish, from a flavor bomb of all the vegetables pulsed in the food processor then added to the sauce, from the lemons, olives, and garlic, and from the final addition of a freshly diced tomato.

SPECIAL EQUIPMENT FOOD PROCESSOR; 5-QUART (5-L) OR LARGER FRENCH OVEN

8 boneless chicken thighs with skin

1 teaspoon kosher or sea salt

1/2 teaspoon black pepper

1 teaspoon garlic powder

1 teaspoon paprika

1 small onion, sliced

2 medium shallots, sliced

1 medium carrot, sliced

1 stalk celery with leaves, sliced

20 large cloves garlic, divided

5 tablespoons (75 ml) extra virgin olive oil, divided

2 tablespoons (15 g) all-purpose flour

2 cups (480 ml) dry white wine

2 cups (480 ml) chicken stock

1/2 small organic lemon, sliced paper thin and then into fingernail-size pieces

2 sprigs fresh rosemary, stemmed and leaves minced, divided

1 large tomato, sliced into small dice, reserving seeds and juice

1 (8-ounce / 115-g) jar pitted whole green olives

1 (8-ounce / 230-g) jar olive bruschetta or olive condite or marinated olive salad

Cooked buttered noodles

PREP

Rinse and pat chicken thighs very dry with paper towels. Generously season with salt, pepper, garlic powder, and paprika.

Place the onion, shallots, carrot, celery and leaves, and 4 cloves garlic into the food processor. Pulse vegetables until finely chopped.

COOK

Heat 3 tablespoons oil in the French oven over medium heat. Place the chicken in, skin side down, and brown until golden and crispy, for about 3 minutes. Turn the chicken over and brown the other side for another 3 minutes. Transfer to a plate.

Pour remaining oil into the French oven and heat over medium heat to shimmering hot. Add the vegetables from the food processor and stir while cooking for 6 minutes. Sprinkle in the flour and stir while cooking for 1 minute. Pour in the wine and stock,

bring to a boil over medium heat, and then reduce to a simmer. Add the chicken, remaining garlic, lemon, and half of the rosemary and cook on a low simmer for 20 minutes. Carefully turn the chicken thighs over and cook for another 10 minutes, or until they are tender. Cook a few minutes longer, if needed.

If you would like a thicker sauce, use a slotted spoon to transfer the chicken and garlic to a plate. Bring the sauce to a boil and cook to reduce to the consistency you like. Put everything back in the sauce.

Stir in the remaining rosemary, tomatoes with their seeds and juice, whole olives, and olive bruschetta. Stir and taste for seasoning, adding more salt and pepper, if needed. Gently reheat the dish and serve over buttered noodles.

IDEAS AND SUGGESTIONS

If you have leftovers, purée to make a delicious soup the next day.

COUNTRY-STYLE PORK AND BEEF WITH LENTILS AND VEGETABLES

Porc et Boeuf à la Paysanne, aux Lentilles et aux Légumes SERVES 4 TO 6

A traditional slow-cooked dish from the Auvergne region in the very heart of France, le petit salé is made from lentils, vegetables, and salted pork and or cured pork belly.

When I make it, I mix it up. I add in beef with the pork, vegetables, and the tiny green lentils du puy, which also come from the Auvergne region where they have been grown for over 2,000 years.

This is a dish that takes very little attention; the only work you have to do is to cut up the vegetables. The French oven does the rest! It takes 1 hour 45 minutes to cook the meat, and another 30 minutes for the vegetables and lentils.

Serve it in large shallow soup bowls and place some Dijon mustard and crusty bread on the table.

SPECIAL EQUIPMENT 5-QUART (5-L) OR LARGER FRENCH OVEN; ALUMINUM FOIL; 4 LARGE SHALLOW SOUP BOWLS

- 2 (8-ounce / 225-g) fresh pork hocks
- 2 pounds (900 g) pork country-style ribs
- 4 (8-ounce / 225-g) center-cut beef shanks
- Salt and pepper, to taste
- 4 carrots, 1 grated and 3 sliced into ½-inch (1.5-cm) pieces
- 3 stalks celery with leaves, sliced and divided, leaves chopped
- 7 large cloves garlic, 4 coarsely chopped and 3 sliced
- 3 medium red potatoes, peeled, sliced into ½-inch (1.5-cm) slices, and then sliced into quarters
- 3 tablespoons (45 ml) olive oil
- All-purpose flour
- 1 small onion, coarsely chopped
- 1 teaspoon dried thyme
- 3 teaspoons dried rosemary, divided
- 8 cracks coarsely ground black pepper, divided
- Water
- 1½ cups (300 g) lentils du Puy (tiny green lentils)
- 1 teaspoon salt
- Crusty bread
- Dijon mustard

PREP

Preheat oven to 400° F (200° C). Rinse all of the meat and pat very dry with paper towels. Sprinkle with salt and pepper.

Toss sliced carrots, 2 stalks sliced celery, sliced garlic, and potatoes into a large a bowl.

COOK

Heat the oil in the French oven over medium heat to shimmering hot, add the pork hocks and brown on all sides. Transfer to a plate. Dredge pork ribs in flour and then brown on all sides. Transfer to a plate. Dredge beef shanks in flour then brown on all sides. Transfer to a plate.

Put all the meat back into the French oven and add the grated carrot, remaining celery, chopped onion, chopped garlic, thyme, 2 teaspoons rosemary, and 4 cracks of pepper. Pour in water to just cover. Bring to a boil, reduce to a simmer, cover, and place in the oven.

Reduce the oven temperature to 325° F (160° C) and cook for 2 hours, turning the meat a couple of times. If the meat is falling-off-the-bone tender, transfer it to carving board. If not, cook another 15 minutes then transfer to the board. Cover loosely with aluminum foil and allow to rest for 10 minutes. Slice off fat and discard. Slice or shred as you would for pulled pork. Discard the bones (do not give bone to pets as they are now soft and apt to chip).

Strain the broth from the French oven into a fine-mesh strainer over a bowl and discard the contents of the strainer. Measure out 5 cups (1.2 l) of broth and pour back into the French oven. Reserve remaining broth.

Add the bowl of carrots, celery, garlic, and potatoes, remaining rosemary, 4 cracks pepper, lentils, and salt to the French oven. Bring to a boil on the stovetop over medium heat then reduce to a simmer and cook for 30 minutes. Taste and add more salt or pepper, if desired. Stir in the chopped celery leaves. Put the meat back into the French oven with the vegetables and stir while gently heating up again.

To serve, divide vegetables, lentils, and meat between the bowls. Spoon some of the remaining broth over the meat to moisten. Serve with crusty bread and Dijon mustard.

IDEAS AND SUGGESTIONS

Use white or red wine instead of water. Leftovers are even better the next day.

BRAISED LAMB SHANKS OSSOBUCO WITH GREMOLATA

Ossobuco d'Agneau Braisé et Gremolata SERVES 4

This recipe provides four people with lovely tender lamb, which you serve with the vegetables it cooks with over pappardelle noodles. It is garnished with minced lemon, lime, parsley, garlic, and grated cheese.

SPECIAL EQUIPMENT 5-QUART (5-L) OR LARGER FRENCH OVEN

- 4 lamb shanks cut about 1½ to 2 inches (4 cm to 5 cm) thick (ossobuco style)
- ¼ cup (30 g) all-purpose flour
- 1 teaspoon salt
- 8 cracks coarsely ground black pepper
- 3 tablespoons (45 ml) extra virgin olive oil
- 4 medium carrots, peeled, 3 cut into 2-inch (5-cm) pieces, and 1 coarsely grated
- 1 medium yellow onion, sliced into thick wedges

- 2 pounds (900 g) small red potatoes, peeled and sliced into quarters
- 8 large cloves garlic, coarsely chopped
- 1 sprig fresh rosemary, stemmed and leaves coarsely chopped
- 3 tablespoons tomato paste
- 1 chicken bouillon cube
- 1 bottle dry white wine
- 3 sprigs fresh thyme, stemmed

- 4 large tomatoes, coarsely chopped reserving seeds and juice
- Grated Parmesan cheese

Gremolata

- 4 wide strips lemon peel, minced
- 5 wide strips lime peel, minced
- 4 tablespoons minced parsley
- 3 tablespoons (15 g) minced garlic
- Salt and pepper, to taste
- 1 tablespoon (15 ml) extra virgin olive oil

PREP

Preheat the oven to 350° F (180° C), rinse lamb shanks, and pat very dry with paper towels.

COOK

Mix the flour, salt, and pepper together. Spread it out on a plate or piece of wax paper then drag the lamb over the flour to dredge both sides. Shake off excess.

Heat oil in the French oven over medium heat. Brown the lamb on all sides. Don't move the meat around too much, let it sear and brown on 1 side before turning over and repeating on the other side.

Next, add the carrot pieces, onion, potatoes, garlic, rosemary, and tomato paste into the French oven. Grate in the bouillon cube. Pour in the wine. Cover and place in the oven to cook for 1 hour. Uncover, turn the shanks over, add the grated carrots, cover, and cook 1 more hour, or until the meat is tender and almost falling off the bone.

Put the French oven on the stovetop over low heat. Stir in the thyme leaves and the tomatoes with their seeds and juice and cook 5 minutes then taste for seasoning, adding more salt and pepper, if desired.

Gremolata

While the lamb is cooking, make the Gremolata. Place the lemon and lime into a bowl. Add the parsley, garlic, salt, pepper, and oil to the bowl and mix well.

To serve, transfer one ossobuco to each plate, surround with vegetables, top with a ladle of sauce, sprinkle with the Gremolata, and serve with a bowl of grated Parmesan cheese.

IDEAS AND SUGGESTIONS

Omit the Gremolata and simply shave big curls of Parmesan over the top.

STEWING

Stews are a satisfying one-pot meal. All I have to do is serve one over egg noodles or polenta or rice and I am done. They are basically prepared the same way a braise would be, only with smaller pieces of meat or poultry, more liquid, and sometimes bigger pieces of vegetables.

Once all the ingredients are in the French oven, they cook themselves. This gives me time to do other things, knowing I have a fabulous meal coming. Ladled over noodles, sprinkled with loads of fresh herbs, and served with a nice wine, stews make a comforting meal to look forward to.

BEEF STEW À LA BORDELAISE, CARAMELIZED CARROTS, AND TURNED POTATOES

Ragoût de Boeuf à la Bordelaise, Carottes Caramélisées et Pommes de Terre Tournées SERVES 6

Bordelaise sauce is made with red wine from Bordeaux, bone marrow, shallots, and butter. It is also a base for a beef stew that I make when I have guests over for dinner because it looks tremendous on the table when served in my copper French oven.

SPECIAL EQUIPMENT 5.5-QUART (5.5-L) OR LARGER; PARCHMENT OR WAX PAPER

3 pounds (1,350 kg) beef chuck, cut into 1-inch cubes

2 grass-fed beef marrow bones (or beef soup bones that have a little meat on them) that fit into the French oven with its lid on

6 medium russet potatoes

1 pound (450 g) pearl or cipollini onions

2 tablespoons (30 ml) extra virgin olive oil, plus more as needed

4 large shallots, finely chopped

¼ cup (30 g) all-purpose flour

1 teaspoon salt, plus more

6 cracks freshly ground black pepper, plus more

4 cups (960 ml) Bordeaux red wine, or any full-bodied dry red wine

¼ cup (60 g) tomato paste, plus 1 tablespoon (15 g)

3 teaspoons sugar

2 teaspoons dried thyme

4 large cloves garlic, coarsely chopped

2 beef bouillon cubes

6 thin medium carrots, peeled and left whole or cut into ½-inch (1.5-cm) pieces

4 tablespoons (60 g) salted butter, divided

⅓ cup (60 g) light brown sugar

½ bunch flat-leaf parsley, coarsely chopped

PREP

Preheat oven to 325° F (160° C). Rinse beef cubes and marrow bones and pat very dry with paper towels.

Peel potatoes with a vegetable peeler then use the peeler to "turn" them, peeling away potato as you turn it, resulting in a smooth oval. Pop them into a bowl of water until ready to cook to keep them from browning.

Drop pearl onions into a saucepan of boiling water and cook for 2 minutes. Drain and peel.

COOK

Heat oil in the French oven over medium heat until it is shimmering hot then add the marrow bones. Brown for 3–4 minutes then remove to a plate. Add the shallots and cook for about 3 minutes. Remove to a plate.

Mix the flour with salt and pepper and spread on a piece of parchment paper. Dredge the meat cubes in the flour, shake off exces. Add a little more oil to the French oven and heat to shimmering hot over medium heat. Add the meat cubes, 1 batch at a time, to the French oven to brown on all sides. Do not move the meat around, giving it time to sear to a crisp golden

continued >

color. Remove browned meat and repeat with remaining meat cubes, adding more oil as needed.

Return all the meat cubes, bones, and shallots back into the pot.

Mix the wine, tomato paste, sugar, thyme, and garlic in a large bowl. Grate in the bouillon cubes then whisk to combine. Pour over the meat, cover, and place in the oven to cook for 2 1/2 hours. Check that the meat is tender. If not, cook another 30 minutes. The last 20 minutes, add the onions.

Meanwhile, cook the potatoes in a medium saucepan with water to cover them by 2 inches (5 cm). Bring to a boil and cook until tender, 15–25 minutes. Keep the water but take the potatoes out and drain them in a colander until ready to use.

Bring the potato water back to a boil, toss in the carrots, and cook for 10–20 minutes until tender. Drain and discard water. Pat the carrots dry with a paper towel. Melt 3 tablespoons (45 g) butter in a skillet with the brown sugar until bubbling hot. Toss in the carrots and cook until the carrots are caramelized and lightly browned.

When the beef is ready, pull out the marrow bones, and if there is still marrow in them, remove it and mash it into the sauce. Discard the bones or, alternatively, you can leave the marrow in them and leave the bones in the stew. Whisk remaining butter into the sauce until it is melted and the sauce is glossy. Tuck the carrots and potatoes into the stew.

To serve, bring the French oven to the table and place on a trivet. Garnish with the parsley.

IDEAS AND SUGGESTIONS

I sometimes toast juniper berries and black peppercorns in the oven then crack them in a mortar and pestle and toss them into the sauce for an added kick and texture. A splash of port at the end, before swirling in the butter, is a lovely addition.

A SUNDAY CASSOULET

Le Cassoulet du Dimanche SERVES 8

Rib-sticking cassoulet, a specialty from southwest France, is typically a slow-baked labor-intensive casserole of beans, meats of some kind, and sausages. When I have time, I prepare it the traditional way. When I don't have time, I prepare this version, which speeds up the process a bit and divides cooking between simmering a while on the stove and finishing cooking in the oven. It is all done in a French oven.

SPECIAL EQUIPMENT FOOD PROCESSOR; 5-QUART (5-L) OR LARGER FRENCH OVEN; BAKING SHEET OR ROASTING PAN

- 12 ounces (350 g) smoked bacon, sliced into 1-inch (2.5-cm) pieces
- 2 large duck breasts, sliced into 1-inch (2.5-cm) pieces with slits sliced into the fat layer
- 8 boneless chicken breasts with skin, sliced in half
- 1 pound (450 g) boneless pork shoulder, cut into 1-inch (2.5-cm) pieces

- 1 medium yellow onion, finely chopped, divided
- 2 tablespoons herbes de Provence, divided
- 8 cracks freshly ground black pepper, divided
- 8 large cloves garlic, coarsely chopped, divided
- 3 (15-ounce / 420-g) cans cannellini beans, drained
- 2 chicken bouillon cubes

- ½ cup (120 ml) water
- 1 (6-ounce / 170-g) can tomato paste
- 1 cup (240 ml) dry white wine
- 8 sausages, garlic or kielbasa, smoked, sweet onion, or fennel, quartered
- 8 slices white bread, processed into crumbs with the food processor

COOK

Cook the bacon in the French oven over medium heat until browned and crisp. Remove bacon to a paper towel. Pour out and discard bacon fat.

Cook the duck in the French oven over medium heat until the fat renders and it turns brown and crispy. Remove to a plate.

Cook the chicken in the duck fat until skin is browned and crispy. Toss the cooked duck back into the French oven on top of the chicken.

In a skillet, cook the pork until lightly browned then toss it into the French oven on top of the duck. Toss half of the bacon in then half of the onion. Sprinkle 1 tablespoon herbes de Provence over the onion. Add 4 cracks pepper. Add half the garlic and 1 can of cannellini beans.

Place bouillon cubes in a glass measuring cup with the water and melt in the microwave for 60 seconds. Pour it into a bowl, mix in the tomato paste, then pour in the wine and mix well to blend. Pour this liquid over everything in the French oven. Add the remaining cannellini beans, the remaining onion and garlic, the remaining herbes de Provence, and then tuck the sausages in. Sprinkle the rest of the bacon on top. Simmer on top of the stove, uncovered, for 30 minutes. Meanwhile, preheat the oven to 375° F (190° C).

Place the French oven on a baking sheet or put it in a roasting pan, spread all the bread crumbs over the top, place in the oven, and bake for 20 minutes. Reduce the heat to 325° F (160° C) and bake for another 30 minutes, or until most of the liquid has been absorbed by the beans. Remove from the oven and allow to rest for 20 minutes before serving.

IDEAS AND SUGGESTIONS

Add any kind of meats or poultry to this basic cassoulet recipe: duck, lamb, goose, turkey, or chicken all work well.

MUSSELS, SHRIMP, SCALLOPS, AND WHITE FISH DIEPPOISE

La Marmite Dieppoise aux Moules, Crevettes,
Coquilles Saint-Jacques et Poissons Blancs SERVES 4

This elegant fish stew is prepared in a style found around Dieppe in Normandy. While Provence's fish stew, bouillabaisse, is brothy and boldly flavored with up to six kinds of fish and shellfish, along the coastline of Normandy in the north of France, fish stew is made with fewer ingredients, simmered with butter, cream, and sometimes hard cider. If you add in lobster, it is called Marmite Dieppoise Royale, which is what I sometimes do for holidays.

There are a few steps to this recipe and it takes some time to prepare, but the end result is lovely. You can do everything earlier in the day, up to the point of cooking the fish filets, so that it will only take you a few minutes to assemble the dish and serve it to your guests or family that evening.

SPECIAL EQUIPMENT 5-QUART (5-L) OR LARGER FRENCH OVEN; 4 BIG SHALLOW SOUP BOWLS

40 mussels

1 thin leek

1 cup (240 ml) dry white wine

2 cups (480 ml) clam juice

24 medium shrimp or 20 large shrimp, peeled and shells reserved

2 tablespoons (30 ml) cognac or brandy

3 tablespoons (45 g) unsalted butter

1 thin carrot, peeled and very thinly sliced

3 large shallots, thinly sliced

1 stalk celery with leaves, very thinly sliced and leaves chopped, divided

4 large cloves garlic, finely chopped

Salt and coarsely ground black pepper, to taste

Pinch of cayenne pepper

½ cup (120 g) heavy cream or crème fraîche

4 (4-ounce / 110-g) white fish filets, either cod, hake, halibut, or sole

4 large sea scallops

2 large egg yolks

1 tablespoon water

Paprika

1 baguette, thickly sliced

PREP

Soak the mussels in cold water for 10 minutes. Clean under running water and pull off beards. Throw away any that are open or that have broken shells. You want mussels that are tightly shut.

Trim the leek and clean insides under running water. Thinly slice the white part of the leek. Very thinly slice some of the green part to use for garnish.

COOK

Place the mussels in the French oven, pour in the wine and clam juice, cover, bring to a boil over medium heat, reduce to a simmer, and wait until the mussels have opened. About 3–5 minutes. Discard any that do not open.

With a slotted spoon, transfer the mussels to a colander and leave the broth in the French oven

as you will be building up its flavor with each step. When the mussels are cool enough to touch, remove them from their shells, place in a bowl, and discard the shells.

Place the shrimp in the broth in the French oven, bring to a boil over medium heat, reduce to a simmer, and cook until the shrimp are just pink. With a slotted spoon, remove the shrimp to the bowl of mussels and keep the broth in the French oven.

Toss the shrimp and mussels in the cognac to coat.

Place the shrimp shells in the broth in the French oven, bring to a boil over medium heat, reduce to a simmer, and cook the shells for 15 minutes. Strain the broth into a large bowl and throw away the shells.

Do not wipe out the French oven. Slice in the butter and melt over medium heat then add the leek,

continued >

carrot, shallots, and celery and cook for 4 minutes. Add the garlic, salt, pepper, and cayenne and cook for 2 minutes. Pour in the reserved broth and the cream. Gently simmer for 10 minutes.

You can make the recipe ahead up to this point earlier in the day, leaving everything in the French oven, covered, and keeping cool until ready to proceed. Cover the mussels and shrimp and refrigerate. Reheat the contents of the French oven before putting the fish in.

Place the fish filets and scallops into the broth, cover, and poach over medium-low heat until just done. Timing will depend upon the size and thickness of the fish and scallops, so check after 2 minutes. Remove the filets and scallops to a dish.

With a fork, beat the egg yolks with the water. Pour into the French oven and continuously whisk over medium-low heat for a minute or so to reheat the broth but not let it boil.

Place the fish filets and scallops back into the broth and top with the mussels and shrimp. Sprinkle with paprika, the chopped celery leaves, and leek. Either bring the French oven to the table or ladle into shallow soup bowls. Serve with warmed crusty slices of baguette to sop up the lovely broth.

POACHED HALIBUT POT-AU-FEU

Pot-au-Feu de Flétan SERVES 4

Pot-au-feu is normally a meal of boiled meats or chicken and vegetables, one that almost every family in France has in their tried-and-true repertoire. I like making a version with fish, first stewing some vegetables then gently cooking halibut over the top until it is just done.

It is finished with a flurry of fine orange zest and has a sauce begging for a slice of baguette.

SPECIAL EQUIPMENT 5-QUART (5-L) OR LARGER FRENCH OVEN; 4 SHALLOW SOUP DISHES

2 leeks

2 tablespoons (30 ml) extra virgin olive oil

1 small white onion, finely chopped

8 fingerling or small potatoes, peeled and sliced into ½-inch (1.5-cm) chunks

3 carrots, sliced into ¼-inch (.5-cm) rounds

1 small fennel, bulb thinly sliced and fronds coarsely chopped and reserved

8 white button or baby bella mushrooms, quartered

2 large cloves garlic, finely chopped

1 teaspoon sea salt

4 cracks coarsely ground black pepper

½ bottle white wine

¼ teaspoon turmeric

1 organic orange, zested and juiced, divided

1 sprig fresh thyme, leaves removed from stem

4 (3-inch-long, 6-ounce / 8-cm-long, 170-g) halibut or cod filets

Olive oil

PREP

Slice off the greenest part the leeks and keep for another use. Wash and dry the light green and white parts and slice into ¼-inch (.5-cm) rounds.

COOK

Heat the oil in the French oven over medium heat until shimmering hot. Add all the vegetables, garlic, salt, and pepper and cook for 7 minutes, stirring frequently. Add the wine, turmeric, half the orange zest, half the orange juice, and thyme leaves. Cover and simmer until the potatoes and carrots are cooked, about 25–30 minutes. Stir halfway through.

Season the fish filets with salt and pepper on each side. Nestle them down into the vegetables in the French oven, slightly submerging, cover, bring to a simmer, and cook, covered, for 5 minutes. Check to see that the fish is cooked to your taste and cook longer, if needed.

Distribute the vegetables into each dish. Lay a piece of halibut on top then ladle the broth around the vegetables. Drizzle a little olive oil over the top of the fish, sprinkle on the remaining orange zest, and garnish with the fennel fronds. Serve with salt and a pepper mill.

IDEAS AND SUGGESTIONS

Salmon, scallops, or shrimp can be used instead of halibut or cod.

CHICKEN IN RIESLING WITH GRAPES AND MUSHROOMS

Poulet au Riesling, Raisins et Champignons SERVES 4

My attention was drawn to an earthenware covered casserole sitting on a long buffet table at a friend's house in the north of France. It had a beautiful hand-painted design that I was drawn to—black with small white flowers. While we talked about its origin and where I could find one, my friend pulled the top off it to reveal her Chicken in Riesling Wine, garnished with whole grapes and tiny mushrooms. I came away with that recipe as well as finding my own earthenware casserole in the town of Soufflenheim before leaving the next day. I also love to make this recipe in a French oven.

This recipe is perfect to make ahead of time because it gets better as it rests, and it works really well as a dish to take to a party.

SPECIAL EQUIPMENT 5-QUART (5-L) OR LARGER FRENCH OVEN; BOX GRATER

- 8 bone-in chicken thighs with skin
- 3 shallots
- 1½ medium carrots
- 1 stalk celery
- 2 tablespoons (30 ml) olive oil
- 3 tablespoons (45 g) unsalted butter
- 4 large cloves garlic, finely chopped

- 1 bottle dry Riesling wine
- 2 teaspoons salt
- 4 cracks coarsely ground black pepper
- 1 tablespoon chopped fresh tarragon
- 3 tablespoons (25 g) all-purpose flour
- ½ cup (120 g) light cream

- 16 red grapes, sliced in half
- 16 green grapes, sliced in half
- 16 white button mushrooms, thickly sliced
- Cooked buttered pappardelle noodles
- 4 tablespoons chopped flat-leaf parsley

PREP

Preheat oven to 325° F (160° C). Rinse chicken and pat very dry with paper towels.

Make a mirepoix by finely chopping the shallots, 1 carrot, and celery and tossing them together in a bowl.

COOK

In the French oven, heat the oil over medium heat until shimmering hot and put in the chicken to brown on all sides. Remove chicken to a plate.

Add the butter to the French oven and melt over medium heat then cook the shallots, carrot, and celery mirepoix mixture for 3 minutes. Add the garlic and cook for 2 minutes.

Add the chicken back into the pot, pour in the Riesling, add salt, pepper, and the tarragon. Bring to a simmer, cover, and cook until chicken is cooked through, for 20–30 minutes. Remove the chicken to a plate.

With a fork, blend the flour with the cream then add to the pot and whisk over medium heat until the sauce is thickened. Grate in the ½ carrot on the large holes of the box grater. Add the grapes and mushrooms. Stir to combine and cook on medium for 3 minutes.

Return the chicken to the pot and taste for seasoning, adding more salt, if desired. Gently stir everything together until coated with the sauce, cook for another minute to reheat the chicken, then serve over noodles. Sprinkle 1 tablespoon parsley over each plate.

IDEAS AND SUGGESTIONS

If you prefer, you can substitute chicken stock for the wine.

BASQUE FISH STEW

Cocotte de Poisson du Pays Basque SERVES 6 TO 8

While the other fish stew included in this chapter is made Dieppoise style, with butter and cream, farther down the western coast of France in Basque country, the fish stew has a spicy red broth, bolstered with fish and wine and vegetables. Its peppery flavor comes from piment d'Espelette, *a paprika from the region, and a little bit of fresh red chili pepper.*

I first had it at a checkered-tablecloth restaurant within sight of the sea, where the chef beguiled me with this fish stew that he served with his wife's warm artichoke bread that I broke into hunks to soak up the broth.

SPECIAL EQUIPMENT FOOD PROCESSOR; 5-QUART (5-L) OR LARGER FRENCH OVEN

- 1 medium yellow onion, sliced into big chunks
- 5 large cloves garlic
- 2 medium red bell peppers, 1 sliced into big chunks and 1 sliced into thin ½-inch (1.5-cm) strips
- 1 small carrot, peeled and cut into big chunks
- ½ small hot red pepper
- 3 tablespoons (45 ml) extra virgin olive oil
- 1 teaspoon kosher or sea salt

- 1 large russet potato, peeled and sliced into ½-inch (1.5-cm) cubes
- 4 cups clam broth (or fish stock if you can find it)
- 2 cup (480 ml) dry white wine
- 2 teaspoons piment d'Espelette (slightly smoky paprika)
- 1 teaspoon sweet paprika
- 1 large tomato, finely chopped reserving seeds and juice, or 12 cherry tomatoes, sliced in half

- 1 pound (450 g) mussels, cleaned and beards removed, discarding any that are not tightly shut or have broken shells
- 2 pounds (900 g) halibut or cod, sliced into 2-inch (5-cm) pieces
- 1 pound (450 g) medium or large shrimp, peeled and deveined
- ½ bunch flat-leaf parsley, leaves removed from stem and finely chopped
- Warm crusty bread

COOK

Place onion, garlic, bell pepper chunks, and carrot into the food processor. Add the hot red pepper and pulse until they are all finely chopped.

Warm the oil in the French oven over medium heat, and when shimmering hot, add the sliced red pepper plus the vegetables from the food processor. Cook on medium until they are tender, about 8 minutes. Add the salt, potato, broth, wine, pimente d'Espelette, and paprika. Cover, bring to a boil over medium heat, reduce to a simmer, and cook until the

potatoes are tender, about 20–30 minutes. Stir and taste. Adjust seasoning with salt or pepper, if desired.

Stir in the tomato with its seeds and juice. Add the mussels, cover, and cook for about 4 minutes, or until they open. Discard any mussels that do not open.

Snuggle the fish pieces and shrimp into the broth and simmer for about 5 minutes, or until they are cooked through. Scatter the top with the parsley. Bring to the table to serve with warm crusty bread.

IDEAS AND SUGGESTIONS

Serve with lemon wedges.

BEEF POT-AU-FEU, DECONSTRUCTED

Pot-au-Feu de Boeuf Déstructuré SERVES 8

All over France, people cook various versions of pot-au-feu *(pot on the fire). In general, it is a meal that can be served in two helpings or at two different times, consisting of a soup, meat or poultry, and vegetables.*

My pot-au-feu is all about the bones. Bone marrow is a healthy fat, mostly unsaturated, and loaded with nutrients. Stewing and roasting with the bones adds deep flavor to a pot-au-feu. As well as having marrow bones in the pot-au-feu, I also roast some. And, as well as stewing the vegetables in the pot-au-feu, I also roast vegetables and serve them with the sliced meats.

This is a hearty big meal for a Sunday dinner. You can go casual and serve it right from the French oven, or you can do what I do and dress it up by presenting it deconstructed on plates brought to the table. Stand up one roasted bone on each plate, arrange the stewed slices of meat in the center of the plate, ladle sauce over them, then add the roasted vegetables on top. I serve mine with slices of toasted baguette to spread the marrow on.

SPECIAL EQUIPMENT BAKING SHEET; ALUMINUM FOIL OR PARCHMENT PAPER; 5-QUART (5-L) OR LARGER FRENCH OVEN; 8 LARGE SHALLOW SOUP BOWLS

8 (3-inch / 8-cm) pieces grass-fed, center-cut beef marrow bones

2 (1-inch / 2.5-cm) pieces grass-fed, center-cut beef marrow bones

2 sprigs fresh thyme

1 sprig fresh rosemary

4 beef short ribs

2½ to 3 pounds (1.2 kg to 1.4 kg) beef brisket

4 medium yellow onions, 1 thinly sliced and 3 cut into chunks

1 large leek, sliced into 1-inch (2.5-cm) pieces

8 whole cloves

24 large cloves garlic, 8 coarsely chopped and 16 whole

2 bay leaves

6 black peppercorns

7 medium carrots, 1 sliced into 1-inch (2.5-cm) pieces and 6 sliced into 2-inch (5-cm) pieces

2 stalks celery with leaves, sliced into 1-inch (2.5-cm) pieces and leaves chopped

1 medium green cabbage, half thinly sliced and half cut into chunks

Coarse kosher or sea salt and coarsely ground black pepper, to taste

8 unpeeled russet potatoes or lots of fingerling potatoes, sliced into ¼-inch (.5-cm) rounds

Olive oil

Thin slices of crusty baguette, lightly toasted

Fleur de sel (like Maldon) to serve in a bowl

Pepper mill

Dijon mustard

PREP

Line baking sheet with aluminum foil or parchment paper. Rinse and pat dry the marrow bones.

Pull leaves off thyme and rosemary sprigs. Discard sprigs. Divide thyme into 2 piles. Coarsely chop rosemary leaves.

COOK

Put the meats and 2 (1-inch / 2.5-cm) marrow bones into the French oven, cover with water, and bring to a boil. Skim the foam from the top and discard. Add the thinly sliced onion, leek, cloves, chopped garlic, bay leaves, peppercorns, sliced 1-inch

continued >

(2.5-cm) carrots, celery, 1 pile thyme leaves, rosemary, and more water, if needed, to cover. Bring to a low simmer and cook, uncovered, for 2 hours. Add the thinly sliced cabbage and salt and cook for another 30 minutes, until all the meat is tender. Taste the broth and add salt and coarsely ground black pepper, if desired. Pull out the cloves and bay leaves and discard. Stir in the second pile of thyme leaves and the chopped celery leaves.

During the last hour, begin to prepare the roasted bones and vegetables.

Arrange a middle and bottom rack in the oven and take out the top rack. Preheat the oven to 450° F (230° C).

Stand up the 3-inch (8-cm) bones on the baking sheet, rub outsides with olive oil, sprinkle with sea salt, and place on the middle shelf of the oven.

Coat the chunks of onions, 2-inch (5-cm) carrots, whole cloves garlic, chunks of cabbage, and potatoes with olive oil then spread them out in a layer on the baking sheet, sprinkle with salt, and place on the bottom shelf of the oven. Bake both bones and vegetables for 15 minutes. Check the bones, and if they are done and the marrow cooked through, remove. Otherwise leave in for another 5 minutes. Remove if they are done and keep warm. Cook the vegetables longer if needed, until they are fork tender.

Meanwhile, remove the meats from the French oven to a cutting board. Slice or pull the meat off the short ribs and slice the brisket against the grain.

To serve, stand up one marrow bone in each bowl, arrange some sliced meat in the center, pour on a little of the broth and add roasted vegetables over the top. Offer warm baguette slices and a small bowl of flaky salt or fleur de sel so that you can spread marrow on slices of the baguette and sprinkle with the salt.

Cover the remaining pot-au-feu (which is now soup), refrigerate, and serve the next day with crusty warm bread.

IDEAS AND SUGGESTIONS

Oxtails add incredible richness to the broth if you would like to use them. If you can find new carrots, either from your garden or farmers market, leave them whole when roasting.

FRYING

Other than having a professional electric fryer with temperature control, I can't imagine owning a more perfect utensil to use for deep-frying than a French oven. Since most people don't have a dedicated electric fryer, having the ability to do deep-frying in the French oven exponentially expands the amount of things you can cook with it.

French ovens heat evenly and are deep enough so that you can fry without fear of being splattered by oil. If you bring the oil back up to temperature after taking fried food out and before putting in the next batch, your food will cook quickly and perfectly without absorbing oil.

I almost always use olive oil for my deep frying. It adds flavor and fries beautifully, because the sweet spot for my frying is around 350–375° F (180–190° C). I use a quart of oil and, after frying with it, allow it to cool. I then decant it into a canning jar with a lid and keep it in the refrigerator to use for another deep-frying adventure.

I love to deep-fry French fries, doughnuts, potato chips, fish filets dredged in seasoned flour, vegetables of all kinds dipped in a light batter, and oysters if I can find big fat plump ones.

NUN'S SIGHS

Soupirs de Nonne MAKES ABOUT 15

I was first served these one summer night in Provence. A huge shallow bowl came to the table filled with little puffs that were spooned into our plates. We picked them up, mere drops that were warm and light as air, to pop into our mouths. It was as if there were a sigh inside when you bit down on them.

Sometimes called pets de nonne, *sometimes* soupirs de nonne, *there are several translations and explanations for the French name for these small fried dough balls, all of which are related in some way to nuns. I like to think of them as* soupirs de nonne— *nun's sighs.*

In France they are made with vanilla, almond, or anise extract or orange flower water. Instead, my secret ingredient is Fiori di Sicilia extract, an ethereal Italian flavoring that I find intriguing for its flowery overtones and hints of vanilla and orange. It is expensive, but you only use a few drops in a recipe as it is quite strong. If you buy a 1-ounce (30-ml) bottle, it will store for a long while in the refrigerator. King Arthur Flour manufactures the one I use the most and it is available from them online. If you wish, you can substitute 1 teaspoon vanilla for the Fiori di Sicilia in this recipe.

SPECIAL EQUIPMENT DEEP-FRYING THERMOMETER WITH A CLIP; 5-QUART (5-L) FRENCH OVEN

Vegetable oil

1 cup (240 ml) milk

⅛ teaspoon salt

2 tablespoons (25 g) sugar

½ teaspoon Fiori di Sicilia extract

5 tablespoons (75 g) unsalted butter, sliced into pats

1 cup (120 g) all-purpose flour

4 large eggs, room temperature

1 organic orange, zested (save juice for another use)

Powdered sugar

COOK

Clip the thermometer to the side of the French oven and fill it with enough vegetable oil to deep-fry. Heat the oil over medium heat to 350° F (180° C).

In a saucepan, whisk the milk, salt, sugar, Fiori di Sicilia extract, and butter until the sugar is dissolved. Keep stirring until the butter is melted and the mixture comes to a boil.

Remove from the heat and pour in the flour all at once. With a wooden spoon, begin to vigorously stir. Put back on medium low and keep stirring for a couple of minutes to cook away moisture and dry out the dough, stirring until it begins to pull away from the sides of the saucepan and forms a ball.

Remove from the heat and vigorously stir in 1 egg at a time. When all eggs are incorporated and the dough looks shiny and elastic, add in the orange zest and beat to combine.

Oil 2 teaspoons. With 1 teaspoon, scoop up some dough and smooth into a round with a finger dipped in water. With the second spoon, push the ball off the spoon into the hot oil. Working in small batches, dropping in 5 or 6 at a time, fry until they are golden brown and puffed. Transfer to a paper towel. Repeat process until the batter is used.

Serve warm with a sifting of powdered sugar.

IDEAS AND SUGGESTIONS

François Payard makes his with cocoa and rum. You can also grate in tart apple or lemon zest or add anise extract rather than vanilla.

SWEET POTATO CHIPS

Frites de Patates Douces SERVES 4

As with making French fries, this is a 2-step process. Put aside a little time on a weekend to make these just for snacking. You will see how easy it is to fry in your French oven and will be inspired to try variations.

SPECIAL EQUIPMENT 4-QUART (4-L) OR LARGER FRENCH OVEN; DEEP-FRYING THERMOMETER WITH A CLIP

2 pounds (900 g) sweet potatoes

Olive oil

Freshly grated Parmesan cheese

PREP

Wash the potatoes and pat very dry with paper towels. Do not peel. Slice very thinly, either with a sharp knife or with a mandolin. Dry the slices very well with paper towels.

COOK

Heat 2 inches (5 cm) olive oil in the French oven to 325° F (160° C). Drop in a few chips at a time and cook until soft, but do not cook them until they are crisp. Keep the oil in the French oven.

With a slotted spoon, remove to paper towels and repeat with the remaining chips.

When you are ready to serve the chips, reheat the oil in the French oven, this time to 360° F (180° C).

Drop in the chips, a few at a time, and fry until golden and crispy. Remove with a slotted spoon to paper towels. Repeat until all chips are cooked.

Toss chips into a big bowl. Sprinkle Parmesan cheese from your hand held about a foot above the chips while you shake the bowl to move the chips around. Or you can shake them with the Parmesan in a brown paper bag. Serve immediately.

IDEAS AND SUBSTITUTIONS

One friend makes these for her children and sprinkles light brown sugar mixed with cinnamon on them, which they love.

CRISPY FRIED SHRIMP

Crevettes Frites SERVES 4

Once I mastered making French fries in my French oven, I watched what my friends were making and continued my education in deep-frying. What they made ranged from deep-fried herbs to vegetables from their garden to tiny cod and potato croquettes to shellfish. Deep-frying large shrimp quickly won out as one of my favorite snacks or meals. I serve them on their own, sprinkled with salt, or with a wedge of lemon.

SPECIAL EQUIPMENT DEEP-FRYING THERMOMETER WITH A CLIP; 5 QUART (5 L) OR LARGER FRENCH OVEN; 2 BAKING SHEETS

Vegetable or olive oil

1 egg

2 tablespoons (30 ml) sparkling water or beer

1¼ teaspoons salt, divided

4 cracks black pepper

½ cup (60 g) all-purpose flour

½ cup (60 g) cornstarch

1½ teaspoons paprika

1 teaspoon ground cumin

Pinch of cayenne pepper

2 tablespoons (15 g) grated Parmesan cheese

40 large shrimp, cleaned, peeled, and dried

Salt and pepper, to taste

Lemon wedges

PREP

Preheat oven to 250° F (120° C) and place a double layer of paper towels on the counter.

COOK

Attach thermometer to the French oven. Pour in 2 inches (5 cm) of oil and heat to 350° F (180° C).

Whisk the egg with the sparkling water or beer, ¼ teaspoon salt, and pepper in a shallow bowl.

Mix together the flour, cornstarch, remaining salt, paprika, cumin, cayenne, and cheese in a large shallow bowl.

Dip the shrimp in the egg mixture then in the flour mixture and place on a baking sheet. You can be generous with the flour mixture. Continue until all shrimp are coated.

Drop a few shrimp into the hot oil to fry until golden, for about 2½ minutes. Transfer to the paper towels to drain for 30 seconds and sprinkle with salt and pepper. Transfer to a baking sheet in the oven to keep warm and repeat with remaining shrimp.

Mound them on a large serving dish and garnish with lemon wedges.

IDEAS AND SUBSTITUTIONS

Try this with any shellfish or sliced pieces of cod or halibut.

LEFTOVER MASHED POTATO CROQUETTES

Croquettes de Purée de Pommes de Terre MAKES 28

This is a retro recipe that I just love. My version uses leftover mashed potatoes (I always make a double batch of mashed potatoes anyway so that I have leftovers) or I make fresh mashed potatoes with the recipe below then cover them and put them in the refrigerator for a day or so to dry out and solidify.

Not only does this method produce better croquettes, but I can make mashed potatoes a day or two ahead and have them ready to go when I want them. I learned this technique from my grandmother who used to do this, and her potato croquettes were legendary. She served hers with a ladle of warm hollandaise sauce draped over them, while I serve mine with a simple tomato sauce for dipping.

I fry the croquettes in a French oven and serve them on paper napkins, but you can also make a dressed salad as a bed for presenting them.

I warn you, these are addictive. They are light as air on the inside with a thin crispy crust on the outside.

SPECIAL EQUIPMENT RICER, FOOD MILL, OR POTATO MASHER; 5-QUART (5-L) OR LARGER FRENCH OVEN; DEEP-FRYING THERMOMETER WITH A CLIP; BAKING SHEET LINED WITH PARCHMENT PAPER

4 medium russet potatoes, peeled and sliced into ½-inch (1.5-cm) cubes	½ teaspoon kosher or sea salt	Vegetable or olive oil
	2 cracks coarsely ground black pepper	½ cup (60 g) all-purpose flour
2 large cloves garlic, minced	¾ cup (80 g) grated Parmigiano-Reggiano cheese	2 eggs, beaten
⅛ teaspoon cayenne pepper		½ teaspoon Dijon mustard
⅛ teaspoon allspice	½ cup (70 g) minced prosciutto	½ cup (75 g) seasoned breadcrumbs

COOK

Toss the potatoes into a saucepan, cover with water, bring to a boil, reduce to a simmer, and cook for about 20 minutes, until fork tender. Drain and let sit in the colander for 10 minutes to allow steam to evaporate and the potatoes to dry out.

Put them through a ricer, a food mill, or mash them in a large bowl. Stir in the garlic, cayenne, allspice, salt, pepper, cheese, and prosciutto. You should have approximately 4 cups (960 ml). At this point, I cover them with plastic wrap and put them in the refrigerator for at least a day or two. If you are using leftover mashed potatoes, you need 4 cups and then mix them with the above ingredients.

When you are ready to make the croquettes, pour at least 2 inches (5 cm) of oil into the French oven, clip on the thermometer, and heat to 350–365° F (175–185° C).

Set up your frying station on a counter near the stove. First, set up a plate with the flour. Next to it, place a plate that has the eggs combined with the mustard and a sprinkle of salt and pepper. And, next to it, place a plate with the breadcrumbs.

Flour your hands, scoop out 2 tablespoons (30 g) of the potato mixture and shape into round balls. Roll them first in the plate of flour and shake off excess. Roll in the plate with the egg mixture then roll in the plate of breadcrumbs. Place on the baking sheet and finish making the remaining balls.

Fry 4 at a time until golden brown, for about 1 ½–2 minutes. Drain on paper towels and sprinkle immediately with salt. Keep warm in a 200° F (90° C) oven, if you wish, until ready to serve.

IDEAS AND SUGGESTIONS

Stuff each with an olive or a small ball of mozzarella. Use Gruyère or a sharp cheddar cheese. Serve with sour cream and applesauce.

Fabrique de Calissons
BECHARD
PATISSIER Les Calissons d'Aix CONFISEUR

DESSERTS IN
MINI COCOTTES

_____

I used to prepare and serve desserts in small white ramekins for years, but when the French oven manufacturers came out with their mini cocottes, I immediately fell in love with them and switched. As I experimented and developed recipes to fit into them, it became clear to me that, because they did everything a white ramekin did, it was really about how they looked and how they elevated the presentation of a dessert that solidly won me over. French mini cocottes come in all materials, including stainless steel, shiny copper with little brass handles, and stoneware and enameled cast iron in so many colors you could match them to any menu or season or decor.

VANILLA PUDDING AND RASPBERRY TARTS

Tartes à la Crème à la Vanille et à la Framboise MAKES 6

Once I learned to make classic French fruit tarts with vanilla pastry cream and a pâte sucrée crust years ago in Paris, I could create almost any size tart with the basic technique and use any berries or fruits that were in season.

When I tried various ways to make one in mini cocottes, the version I liked the best was when I used sheets of phyllo dough instead of making the traditional sugar crust for them. This one has the pudding cradled inside a delicate baked phyllo flower. I place just one perfect raspberry on top.

SPECIAL EQUIPMENT 6 MINI COCOTTES; ROASTING PAN; PASTRY BRUSH; 4-QUART (4-L) FRENCH OVEN OR VERY LARGE SAUCEPAN; STAND MIXER

Phyllo crust

1 roll from a package of frozen phyllo pastry, thawed

2 tablespoons (30 g) unsalted butter, melted

Sugar

Filling

3 cups (720 ml) milk, room temperature

3 cups (720 ml) half-and-half, room temperature

¼ teaspoon salt

3 teaspoons vanilla extract

1 teaspoon almond extract

8 large egg yolks, room temperature

1¼ cups (250 g) sugar

½ cup (60 g) cornstarch

2 tablespoons (15 g) all-purpose flour

4 tablespoons (60 g) unsalted butter

6 raspberries

Powdered sugar

PREP

Preheat oven to 350° F (180° C), lightly butter cocottes, and place in roasting pan.

COOK

Phyllo Crust

On a clean work surface, separate 6 sheets of phyllo, and return the remaining sheets to the freezer. Stack the sheets and, with kitchen scissors, cut them in half so that you have 9 x 7-inch (23 x 18-cm) pieces.

With a pastry brush, lightly brush 1 sheet with the melted butter. Take another sheet, turn it around the other way, lay it on top, and brush with melted butter. Gently lift the 2 sheets and carefully scrunch them down into a cocotte so that they touch the bottom and have a pretty overhang of "leaves" around the edges. Repeat this process with the remaining cocottes. Sprinkle the phyllo interiors and leaves with sugar.

Bake in the oven for 3–7 minutes, or until golden and crispy. Watch them as they will brown quickly. This step can be done ahead and they can be kept at room temperature until ready to use.

Filling

Heat the milk, half-and-half, salt, vanilla extract, and almond extract in the French oven over medium heat, until simmering. Turn the heat down to very low.

In the stand mixer, beat the egg yolks and sugar together for 3–4 minutes until very thick. Sift in the cornstarch and flour then beat to incorporate.

Bring the milk mixture back to almost scalding. With a measuring cup, carefully pour a third of the hot milk into the egg mixture with the machine running. Then pour all of the egg mixture into the hot milk in the French oven and cook over low heat while you constantly whisk. It will look frothy and thick. You will be doing this for at least 5 minutes, as you want the pudding to become thick enough to hold its shape.

When you like the consistency, slice in the butter, whisking until it is all melted. Cool the pudding to room temperature. If you are using it later, cover with plastic wrap touching the top and put it in the refrigerator.

When you are ready to assemble the tarts, spoon the pudding into the shells in the cocottes and top with one raspberry. If you wish, you can sift a little powdered sugar over the top of each.

IDEAS AND SUGGESTIONS

Drizzle the top with melted white chocolate: melt white chocolate morsels in the top of a double boiler then, using a fork, lift up some and drizzle back and forth over the raspberry.

Slice ripe bananas into the bottom of the cocottes before filling with pudding. Top with chopped bananas.

BUTTERSCOTCH POTS DE CRÈME

Pots de Crème au Caramel MAKES 6

A simple rosette of whipped cream in the center of each is all you need for these pots de crème. There's a hint of salt in there somewhere, an echo of childhood, then a realization that you can be a grown-up and find renewed pleasure in the now silky and sophisticated version of the butterscotch pudding before you. Spoon poised? Dip in.

SPECIAL EQUIPMENT 6 MINI COCOTTES; ROASTING PAN; ALUMINUM FOIL

4 cups (960 g) heavy cream

6 tablespoons (90 g) unsalted butter

1½ tablespoons (25 ml) vanilla extract

2 cups (360 g) dark brown sugar

½ cup (90 g) light brown sugar

1 teaspoon kosher salt

8 large egg yolks

Sweetened whipped cream

PREP

Preheat oven to 325° F (160° C) and bring water to a boil that you will later add to the roasting pan.

COOK

In a sturdy saucepan, combine the cream, butter, vanilla, dark brown sugar, light brown sugar, and salt. Bring to a boil then reduce to a simmer and cook for 4 minutes, whisking until the sugar is dissolved.

In a large bowl, whisk the egg yolks then slowly pour in some of the hot cream while whisking to combine. Then pour this mixture back into the pan and whisk well.

Place the cocottes into the roasting pan then divide the butterscotch mixture between them. Pour the boiling water in the roasting pan so it reaches halfway up the cocottes, cover the roasting pan with aluminum foil, then put it into the oven and bake for 45 minutes. Cooking time will depend on the temperature of the cream mixture by the time you put it in the cocottes. They are done when they are set around the edges but still have a little wiggle in the middle.

Let them cool to room temperature then place in the refrigerator to chill for at least 6 hours. Serve with a little whipped cream in the center.

IDEAS AND SUGGESTIONS

Place a dollop of dark chocolate ganache on top with whipped cream and a few Maldon salt flakes. Try adding some crumbled amaretti cookies on top, or, place 1 tablespoon (15 ml) Scotch Whiskey in the bottom of each before spooning in the pudding.

INDIVIDUAL CHOCOLATE FONDUE

Fondues au Chocolat Individuelles MAKES 6

There's a hole-in-the-wall tiny restaurant on a back street in Nice that makes individual chocolate fondues. Life is good when their fruit is ripe, bursting with juice, and the melting dark chocolate is plentiful enough to evoke a surge of happiness when it is finished.

The experience can be recaptured at home when served hot in mini cocottes that are surrounded by the best fruit you can find. It takes all of 10 minutes to make. But don't stop with fruit. Banana cake, coconut macaroons, mini pretzels, lady fingers, or cubes of gingerbread are all terrific dunked into melted chocolate. N'est-ce pas?

SPECIAL EQUIPMENT 6 MINI COCOTTES

Dippers

Strawberries, thickly sliced

Kiwi, thickly sliced

Bananas, thickly sliced

Cantaloupe balls

Blood orange or Cara Cara orange, thickly sliced

Fondue

3 cups (720 g) heavy cream

3 (3.5-ounce / 100-g) bars 70 percent bittersweet chocolate, broken into pieces

1 ½ teaspoons vanilla extract

½ teaspoon salt

½ cup (60 g) Hershey's Special Dark Cocoa

2 tablespoons (25 g) sugar

6 teaspoons (30 ml) raspberry liqueur

2 tablespoons (30 g) unsalted butter

COOK

Dippers

Attractively arrange dippers on 6 plates so they are ready to serve as soon as the melted chocolate is ready. Each plate will have a selection of dippers.

Fondue

In a saucepan, heat the cream to a simmer. Add the chocolate and whisk until melted. Add the vanilla, salt, cocoa, sugar, and liqueur and whisk until well blended. Just before serving, whisk in the butter then pour into the cocottes.

Serve each cocotte with a plate of dippers.

IDEAS AND SUGGESTIONS

Use Lindt's Extreme Orange Chocolate Bars and Cointreau; Toblerone chocolate and Amaretto Liqueur; or Lindt's Mint Chocolate Bars with Mint Liqueur.

For children, make it with milk chocolate and serve with marshmallows, animal crackers, and small brownie squares. You can also melt in ½ cup creamy peanut butter or raspberry jam.

LEMON LOVERS' PANNA COTTA WITH LEMON CURD

Panna Cotta à la Crème au Citron pour les Amoureux du Citron MAKES 6

Every year in the city of Menton in the south of France they celebrate the lemons that grow there with a festival of floats made out of lemons and oranges and with an exhibition of products made with citrus. It is a way of looking forward out of the winter and into the summer sun and a reminder to use oranges and lemons in the dishes you make. One of the first I would make were bottles of limoncello, then a lovely lemon soup with chicken and rice, and then, of course, a lemon tart or lemony panna cotta.

My lemon panna cotta is an easy no-bake dessert that is light and fresh tasting. Serve it with a dollop of lemon curd and a mint leaf, or add a little amaretto cookie or a pine nut cookie, and side with a shot glass of chilled limoncello.

SPECIAL EQUIPMENT 6 MINI COCOTTES; STAND MIXER

Panna Cotta

4 cups (960 g) heavy cream

¹⁄₂ cup (100 g) plus 2 tablespoons (25 g) sugar

1 tablespoon (10 g) unflavored gelatin

1 organic lemon, finely zested and juiced, about 2 tablespoons (10 ml) juice

3 teaspoons (15 ml) lemon extract

¹⁄₂ teaspoon vanilla extract

Lemon Curd

3 large egg yolks, room temperature

¹⁄₂ cup (100 g) plus 3 tablespoons (35 g) sugar

3 organic lemons, finely zested and juiced, about ¹⁄₃ cup (80 ml) juice

4 tablespoons (60 g) unsalted butter

6 mint leaves

COOK

Panna Cotta

Heat the cream and sugar in a saucepan and bring to a boil. Take off the heat and whisk in the gelatin then bring back to a gentle simmer and whisk for 5 minutes to dissolve the gelatin.

Add the lemon zest, lemon juice, lemon extract, and vanilla extract and bring back to a simmer.

Take off the heat and pour into the cocottes. Cool to room temperature then cover with plastic wrap and place in the refrigerator to chill for at least 3 hours.

Lemon Curd

In a saucepan, bring 2 inches (5 cm) of water to a simmer.

In the bowl of the stand mixer, beat the eggs, sugar, lemon zest, and lemon juice together until pale and thick, about 2 minutes.

Pour egg mixture into a heatproof bowl and place over the pot of simmering water. You can also use a double boiler if you like. Whisk continually until the mixture thickens, anywhere from 10–15 minutes.

Take off the heat, slice in the butter, and whisk until it melts and the curd is well blended. Cool to room temperature, cover with plastic wrap so that it touches the lemon curd, and refrigerate until ready to use.

To serve the panna cotta, dollop lemon curd over the top of each cocotte and insert a mint leaf. Serve any extra lemon curd in a separate bowl.

IDEAS AND SUGGESTIONS

Use Cara Cara or blood oranges for a beautiful color. Use buttermilk, coconut, or almond milk instead of cream.

BANANA RICE PUDDING

Gâteau de Riz à la Banane MAKES 6

The only way I can think of to improve this creamy banana rice pudding is to spoon some warm Bananas Foster (sliced bananas sautéed in butter, sugar, rum, and cinnamon) over each cocotte. Otherwise, serving it warm or chilled on its own is sufficiently worthy of a special occasion. For me, that is any night with loved ones and friends.

SPECIAL EQUIPMENT 6 MINI COCOTTES; ROASTING PAN; 3- TO 5-QUART (3- TO 5-L) FRENCH OVEN; FOOD PROCESSOR; PARCHMENT PAPER

1 cup (200 g) sugar

2 cups (480 ml) water, plus 1 tablespoon (15 ml)

1 cup (190 g) basmati rice

1 ripe banana

¼ cup (45 g) dark brown sugar

2 teaspoons vanilla extract

1½ cups (360 ml) half-and-half

2 large egg yolks

¼ cup (50 g) sugar, plus 2 tablespoons (25 g)

¼ teaspoon ground cinnamon

Chilled whipped cream, optional

PREP

Preheat oven to 325° F (160° C) and bring water to a boil that you will later add to the roasting pan. Place cocottes in the roasting pan.

COOK

To make the caramel, heat sugar and 1 tablespoon (15 ml) water over medium heat in a saucepan and stir to mix. Then leave alone over heat until the sugar begins to melt and take on a golden color. Stir to dissolve the sugar crystals then leave to cook, watching carefully. When it begins to bubble up and turn brown, take off the heat and carefully pour into each cocotte. Do not let the hot sugar syrup get on your skin. Move the cocottes around to coat with the syrup up the sides as well.

To make the rice pudding, pour 2 cups (480 ml) water into the French oven, bring to a boil over medium heat, and then pour in the rice. Reduce to a simmer, cover, and cook on low for 20 minutes. Stir once in a while. Take off the heat, leaving the lid on, and let set for 10 minutes.

Meanwhile, slice the banana into the food processor and add the brown sugar and vanilla. Process just until you have a purée.

In a bowl, whisk together the half-and-half, egg yolks, sugar, cinnamon, and banana purée then pour into the rice. Stir to completely mix and bring to a simmer. Cook, continuously stirring, for 2 minutes.

Spoon the rice pudding into each cocotte. Pour boiling water halfway up around the cocottes, place a big sheet of parchment paper over the top, and put the roasting pan in the oven. Bake for 20 minutes.

Cool until you can touch the cocottes then serve warm or chilled with whipped cream.

NO-MACHINE-NEEDED CHOCOLATE ICE CREAM

Crème glacée au Chocolat sans Sorbetière MAKES 6

When I was a teenager I used to make a pretty admirable iced dessert by simply pouring a layer of sweetened heavy cream into the bottoms of metal ice cube trays then pouring fresh orange juice over the top and freezing. Now I make iced desserts in the more glamorous mini cocottes. This one, as my orange and cream creation, does not require an ice cream machine.

Use the best quality chocolate you can find to make this ice cream, it's worth it. Serve with a hot fudge or caramel sauce, a wiggle of whipped cream, and maybe a cherry on top and you're living a chocolate dream.

SPECIAL EQUIPMENT STAND MIXER; 6 MINI COCOTTES; ALUMINUM FOIL

- 2 cups (480 g) heavy cream, chilled
- 1 (14-ounce / 400-g) can sweetened condensed milk
- 6 ounces (170 g) semisweet chocolate, broken into small pieces
- 1 teaspoon vanilla extract
- 1 teaspoon ground cinnamon
- 2 tablespoons (15 g) Hershey's Special Dark Cocoa

COOK

Using the stand mixer, beat the cream until stiff peaks form. Refrigerate.

Combine the condensed milk, chocolate, vanilla, cinnamon, and cocoa in a saucepan, and over very low heat, stir until the chocolate is melted. Refrigerate for 5 minutes.

Fold the chocolate mixture into the whipped cream and spoon into the cocottes. Cover each with aluminum foil and freeze until firm. Serve straight from the freezer, allowing 5 minutes to soften.

IDEAS AND SUGGESTIONS

Chop up slivered almonds or chop hazelnuts and fold in before freezing. Add 2 tablespoons orange liqueur to the chocolate mixture before freezing.

CHRISTMAS EVE WHITE CHOCOLATE MOUSSE WITH MACADAMIA NUT BRITTLE

Mousse de la Veillée de Noël au Chocolat Blanc, Nougatine de Noix de Macadamia MAKES 6

White tends to dominate my decorating around the Christmas holidays. I make a white frosted fruitcake to resemble a wreath, a white soup with ruby red and green garnish (White Soup with Pomegranate Seeds and Pistachios, page 52), traditional white eggnog, and this White Chocolate Mousse for Christmas Eve dinner.

It has to be one of the easiest desserts I make and can be served right away, so I prepare it just before guests and family arrive. The brittle is a fun garnish but it is totally optional since this mousse stands well on its own with only a simple grating of fresh nutmeg.

Remember to use a really good quality white chocolate, checking the ingredients to make sure cocoa butter is in it.

SPECIAL EQUIPMENT CANDY THERMOMETER; SILPAT OR BAKING SHEET WITH PARCHMENT PAPER; STAND MIXER; 6 MINI COCOTTES

Brittle

1½ cups (300 g) sugar

1 teaspoon vanilla extract

1 teaspoon ground cinnamon

Pinch of fleur de sel or salt flakes (optional)

1 stick (115 g) salted butter

1 cup (125 g) roasted salted macadamia nuts

Mousse

2½ cups (600 g) heavy cream, chilled, divided

2 tablespoons (30 ml) white rum or bourbon

1 teaspoon vanilla extract

1½ teaspoons allspice

12 ounces (340 g) best quality white chocolate, finely ground

Freshly grated nutmeg

COOK

Brittle

Pour the sugar, vanilla, cinnamon, and salt into a saucepan and cook over medium heat until the sugar begins to melt. Gently swirl the pan a few times to help it along. Very careful not to spatter yourself, slice in the butter and stir to combine until the candy thermometer reads 300° F (150° C). Toss in all of the nuts and stir.

Pour onto the silpat or baking sheet, spread out with a rubber spatula, and let cool. At this point you can either break it up into 6 pieces or into big chunks to decorate or serve with each cocotte.

Mousse

In a medium saucepan, heat ¾ cup (180 g) cream, rum, vanilla, and allspice until little bubbles form around the edges. Toss in all of the chocolate at once, wait 30 seconds, then turn off the heat and whisk the mixture until completely melted. Cool to room temperature. It will have taken on a darkish color, but that will disappear later when you fold it into the whipped cream.

Meanwhile, whip the remaining cream on medium to medium-high speed until it holds its shape in soft peaks.

Fold a fourth of the whipped cream into the white chocolate mixture then fold in the rest until well combined. Evenly divide among the mini cocottes, serve right away, or refrigerate until ready to use.

Garnish with freshly grated nutmeg and stick a piece of brittle into each one.

IDEAS AND SUGGESTIONS

For the holidays, crush candy canes to sprinkle over the top or tuck a gingerbread cookie into the side. Instead of heating $^1/_2$ cup (120 g) heavy cream, try heating $^1/_2$ cup (120 ml) Bailey's Irish Cream or white chocolate liqueur to melt the chocolate.

Add chopped dried cherries, apricots, or cranberries to the brittle. Or, instead of making brittle, garnish with one strawberry dipped in dark chocolate.

FRESH ORANGE CRÈME CARAMEL

Crème Caramel à l'Orange Fraîche MAKES 6

My neighbor in the south of France used to walk over and pick oranges from my tree then return in the early evening with an orange crème caramel. My oranges were bitter, but she magically transformed that flavor into an edgy but delicious dessert. She would make one for her family and bring me one.

Using regular oranges, or Cara Cara or blood oranges, produces a fresh tasting tender crème caramel that is equally delicious right out of the oven or chilled. Either way, it is beautiful when prepared and served in mini cocottes.

SPECIAL EQUIPMENT ROASTING PAN; CITRUS MICROPLANE; 6 MINI COCOTTES

2 medium organic oranges	2 large egg whites, room temperature	¼ teaspoon vanilla extract
2¼ cups (450 g) sugar, divided	3 cups (720 ml) milk, room temperature	1 tablespoon orange zest
6 large eggs, room temperature	¼ teaspoon salt	2 tablespoons (30 ml) Grand Marnier or other quality orange liqueur

PREP

Preheat oven to 300° F (150° C) and bring water to a boil that you will later add to the roasting pan. Place cocottes in the roasting pan.

Microplane 1 orange to get 1 tablespoon fine orange zest. Juice both oranges to yield 1 cup (240 ml) orange juice.

COOK

To make the caramel sauce, heat 1 cup (200 g) sugar over medium-low heat in a heavy saucepan. Once it begins to liquefy, stir until smooth and melted. Stop stirring and allow the mixture to bubble around the edges and turn a clear dark amber color. Very careful not to burn your skin, pour the hot syrup into each cocotte, swirl, and allow to harden.

To make the custard, place the eggs and egg whites in a large bowl and whisk well. Add remaining sugar and whisk to blend. Pour in the milk and add the salt, vanilla, orange zest, orange juice, and Grand Marnier and whisk to combine.

Pour custard into the cocottes and pour the boiling water into the roasting pan to reach halfway up the cocottes. Place the roasting pan in the oven to bake for 55–60 minutes, or until the custards are just set. If you are going to serve them warm, let them rest for 15 minutes. If you are going to serve them chilled, cool to room temperature then chill for 4 hours.

To serve, garnish each with anything you would like. I love a paper-thin slice of orange that has been diced to garnish the tops and echo the fresh orange flavor of the custard below.

IDEAS AND SUGGESTIONS

Skip the orange flavorings and add in ½ teaspoon more vanilla extract and finely ground candied ginger.

RASPBERRY CLAFOUTIS WITH FUNNELED WARM ICE CREAM

Clafoutis à la Framboise, Coeur de Glace à la Vanille Tiède MAKES 6

For this recipe, melted ice cream is poured through a funnel inserted into the center of just-baked clafoutis so that, when you begin to eat it, you have the coolness of the ice cream playing off the warm dough inside for a delightful flavor and temperature combination.

Clafoutis are desserts made in the Limousin region of France that are made with cherries. I like to pile fresh raspberries at the bottom of the cocottes instead then top it with the batter and bake.

SPECIAL EQUIPMENT BAKING SHEET; 6 MINI COCOTTES; STAND MIXER; SMALL FUNNEL; FINE-MESH TEA STRAINER

Butter, room temperature	1 teaspoon vanilla extract	1¾ teaspoons baking powder
5 tablespoons (65 g) sugar, plus more to coat cocottes	1 teaspoon almond extract	12 tablespoons (100 g) vanilla ice cream
6 ounces (170 g) fresh raspberries	¼ teaspoon salt	Powdered sugar
3 large eggs, room temperature	⅛ teaspoon freshly grated nutmeg	
1¼ cups (300 ml) half-and-half	½ cup (60 g) all-purpose flour	

PREP

Preheat oven to 350° F (180° C). Generously butter the cocottes, coat with sugar, and shake out excess. Place on baking sheet.

COOK

Evenly divide the raspberries between the cocottes, creating a layer at the bottom of each. Reserve 6 raspberries for garnish.

In the bowl of the stand mixer, add the eggs and beat on high for 4 minutes. Beat in the 5 tablespoons (65 g) sugar. Add the half-and-half, vanilla extract, almond extract, salt, and nutmeg and beat to combine.

Sift in the flour and baking powder and beat to combine. Pour this mixture over the raspberries in each cocotte, filling them as high as possible to the top. Place them in the oven and bake for 22 minutes, until puffed and golden brown.

Meanwhile, melt the ice cream until it is liquefied, either in a microwave for 40 or more seconds, or on the stove. Reserve.

Take cocottes out of oven and cool until you can touch them without burning your fingers. Insert the funnel into the center of each, pouring in ice cream until it just hits the top of the clafoutis.

To serve, place one raspberry over the funnel hole of each clafoutis. With a fine-mesh tea strainer, shake powdered sugar over the top of each. Serve warm.

IDEAS AND SUGGESTIONS

To save calories, use fat free half-and-half. It will still taste wonderful. Make with blueberries, plums, or fresh black cherries.

VANILLA CHEESECAKES WITH FRESH STRAWBERRY COMPOTE

Cheesecakes à la Vanille, Compote de Fraises Fraîches MAKES 6

A French cheesecake, made with fromage blanc, *is lighter and less sweet than other cheesecakes, and it is often served with fresh berries. This one is a bit heavier, with a hint of vanilla, almond, and lemon, and is topped with a fresh strawberry and just-made strawberry compote.*

SPECIAL EQUIPMENT ROASTING PAN; STAND MIXER; 6 MINI COCOTTES

3 (8-ounce / 225-g) packages cream cheese, room temperature

1¼ cups (250 g) sugar, divided

2 tablespoons (15 g) all-purpose flour

3 teaspoons vanilla extract

½ teaspoon almond extract

3 tablespoons (45 ml) fresh lemon juice

½ cup (120 g) sour cream

3 large eggs, room temperature

2 cups (350 g) sliced strawberries, plus 6 large strawberries

PREP

Preheat oven to 325° F (160° C) and bring water to a boil that you will later add to the roasting pan. Place cocottes in the roasting pan.

COOK

Slice the cream cheese into the bowl of the stand mixer, add in 1 cup (200 g) sugar, and beat for at least 3 minutes until well blended and fluffy, scraping down the sides of the bowl once. Then beat at high speed for a couple of minutes. Sift in the flour, add the vanilla extract, almond extract, lemon juice, and sour cream, and beat to blend. Beat in the eggs, 1 at a time.

Make the strawberry compote by placing the sliced strawberries into a saucepan and adding the remaining sugar. Crush with a potato masher or fork and cook over medium heat until the berries are broken down and thickened. Cool the strawberry compote to room temperature, cover, and chill until ready to use.

Spoon the cheesecake mixture into the cocottes until they are almost full. Pour the boiling water around them until it reaches halfway up the cocottes and bake for 35 minutes, until set. Cool to room temperature then chill at least an hour.

To serve, spoon some of the strawberry compote over the cheesecakes then garnish with a strawberry. Offer remaining strawberry compote in a small jar or bowl.

IDEAS AND SUGGESTIONS

To make chocolate dipped strawberries to garnish: melt ½ cup (80 g) semisweet chocolate chips with 1 teaspoon vegetable oil in a heatproof bowl set over a pot of simmering water. Stir with a silicon spatula to smooth out. Transfer bowl to kitchen counter, dip the bottom halves of the 6 strawberries into the chocolate, shake off excess, place on baking sheet lined with parchment paper and let set for 5 minutes. Then refrigerate until ready to use, for at least 15 minutes.

DESSERTS IN FRENCH OVENS

Why do I make desserts in the larger French ovens? Because I absolutely love the effect of carrying them to the table and serving a warm, just-out-of-the-oven dessert with a scoop of ice cream over the top. While mini cocottes are perfect for presenting dessert in an elegant way, the large French ovens provide just the opposite, a way of preserving the integral hominess of a communal dessert with no pretense other than to deliver a smile.

WARM APPLE ALMOND CRUMBLE WITH SALTED BUTTERSCOTCH SAUCE

Crumble Tiède aux Pommes et aux Amandes, Sauce Caramel au Beurre Salé

SERVES 6 TO 8

As soon as you make the crumble part of this recipe you will smell the almonds, because you will be massaging a whole package of sweet almond paste into the flour and butter that will bake over the top of the apples.

Below, you will have an apple pie. Above, a crunchy topping just begging for a scoop of ice cream to melt down and trickle into the mass of warm apples below.

SPECIAL EQUIPMENT 5-QUART (5-L) FRENCH OVEN; PASTRY CUTTER; BAKING SHEET

Almond Crumble Topping

1¹/₂ cups (180 g) all-purpose flour

¹/₂ cup (90 g) plus 2 tablespoons (25 g) light brown sugar

1 teaspoon cinnamon

¹/₄ teaspoon salt

1 (7-ounce / 200-g) box almond paste, coarsely grated or broken into crumbs

2 sticks (225 g) unsalted butter, chilled

Filling

2 organic lemons, zested and juiced

12 Granny Smith apples, peeled, cored, and sliced into ¹/₈-inch (.5-cm) pieces

2 teaspoons vanilla extract

4 tablespoons (30 g) all-purpose flour

¹/₂ cup (100 g) sugar

¹/₂ cup (90 g) light brown sugar

2 teaspoons cinnamon

1 teaspoon ground nutmeg

4 tablespoons (60 g) unsalted butter

Salted Butterscotch Sauce

1¹/₂ cups (270 g) dark brown sugar

³/₄ cup (180 g) heavy cream

6 tablespoons (90 g) unsalted butter

1 tablespoon vanilla extract

1 teaspoon kosher or sea salt

PREP

Preheat the oven to 350° F (180° C) and butter the bottom of the French oven.

Fill a large bowl with water. Pour half of the lemon juice into the water and place the apples into the bowl to keep from them browning.

COOK

Almond Crumble Topping

In a large bowl, mix together the flour, brown sugar, cinnamon, salt, and almond paste. Slice in the butter and, using the pastry cutter or using your fingers, work the flour mixture until it looks like crumbs.

continued >

Filling

In a small bowl, combine the remaining lemon juice and vanilla.

In another bowl, mix together the flour, sugar, brown sugar, cinnamon, and nutmeg.

Remove the apples from the bowl of water and pat very dry. Wipe out the bowl they were in, toss the apples back in the bowl, pour in the lemon juice and vanilla mixture, and toss well to coat. Sprinkle the flour and sugar mixture over the apples, toss to coat, then pour the apples into the French oven. Sprinkle the topping all over the top of the apples then slice small pieces of the butter over the top.

Place the French oven on the baking sheet and bake 1 hour, until it is bubbling and golden brown.

Salted Butterscotch Sauce

While the apple crumble is baking, make the sauce. Whisk all the ingredients together in a saucepan over medium heat until it comes to a boil then let it cook for a couple of minutes until it thickens. Allow to cool before pouring into a serving pitcher or bowl.

Serve the warm apple crumble with a pitcher of the caramel sauce to pour over the top.

IDEAS AND SUGGESTIONS

Add cranberries, pears, or plums to the apples. Combine different varieties of apples with sliced strawberries and rhubarb.

WARM CHOCOLATE SEMOLINA SPOON CAKE

Fondant Tiède au Chocolat et à la Semoule SERVES 6 TO 8

This homey chocolate cake is baked right in the French oven. It will rise about halfway up and have a lot of flavor, will be light as air, and have a delightful texture that comes from using semolina in the batter. It's a spoon cake. You serve it with a large serving spoon as you would a pudding.

If I plan on bringing it to the table with ice cream, I pile fresh raspberries and sliced strawberries in the center and dust them with powdered sugar. It's also fantastic with mounds of softly whipped and lightly sweetened heavy cream.

SPECIAL EQUIPMENT STAND MIXER; 4.25- TO 5-QUART (4.25- TO 5-L) FRENCH OVEN

2 cups (480 g) half-and-half

½ teaspoon vanilla extract

½ teaspoon almond extract

½ cup (100 g) superfine sugar plus 1 tablespoon, divided

1 cup (160 g) semisweet chocolate chips

¾ cup (90 g) Hershey's Special Dark Cocoa

¼ cup (40 g) plus 2 tablespoons (20 g) Bob's Red Mill semolina flour

4 large eggs, separated, room temperature

2 large egg whites

1 teaspoon fresh lemon juice

Powdered sugar

Ice cream

PREP

Preheat oven to 350° F (180° C). Generously butter the French oven and coat with sugar on the bottom and all the way up the sides.

COOK

In a saucepan, bring the half-and-half, vanilla extract, almond extract, ¼ cup (50 g) sugar, chocolate chips, and cocoa to a simmer while whisking. When thoroughly melted and blended, whisk in the semolina and bring almost to a boil, continuously whisking until it thickens, about 3 minutes. Take off the heat and allow to cool to room temperature.

Then beat the yolks with a fork into the chocolate semolina mixture until well blended.

Using the stand mixer, beat the egg whites with lemon juice until they begin to hold their shape. Sprinkle in remaining sugar and beat until just stiff.

Err on the side of under whipping, you don't want your whites rigid or dry.

Fold a third of the egg whites into the semolina mixture. Then add the rest and gently fold in. Don't over fold; it is fine if streaks remain.

Scoop into the French oven then run a knife around in the middle to make a circle. Place in the oven and bake for 35 minutes, until set and puffed and cooked through.

Sift powdered sugar over the top and immediately bring to the center of the table with a large serving spoon. Serve from the French oven with a scoop of ice cream on the side.

IDEAS AND SUGGESTIONS

Try serving with rum raisin ice cream and a little rum drizzled over the ice cream.

POACHED PEARS, ROSEMARY CHOCOLATE SAUCE, BLUE CHEESE WEDGE

Poires Pochées, Sauce Chocolat au Romarin, Fromage Bleu SERVES 8

Over the years I have used the classic French recipe for wine poached pears and made it in different ways, finally settling on this rendition. I love taking the poaching liquid from the pears and mixing it with chocolate and rosemary for a warm chocolate sauce to dip the pears into. And I love serving it with a wedge of creamy blue cheese. Tasting a slice of pear with a slice of blue cheese is lovely, and dipping a slice of pear into the chocolate a delightful contrast.

It is best if you make the pears a day ahead and assemble the dessert the next day, because the longer they sit in the poaching liquid the deeper a ruby color they take on.

SPECIAL EQUIPMENT 4- TO 5-QUART (4- TO 5-L) FRENCH OVEN

Pears

8 Anjou pears

1 bottle Cabernet Sauvignon, Pinot Noir, or other dry red wine

2 teaspoons vanilla extract or seeds from 1 vanilla pod

¼ cup (50 g) sugar

1 cinnamon stick, broken

2 whole cloves

1 teaspoon ground nutmeg

3 tablespoons (60 g) blackberry jam

Chocolate Sauce

1 cup (240 ml) poaching liquid

1 cup (240 ml) port wine

¼ cup (50 g) sugar

1 tablespoon chopped fresh rosemary leaves

1 (3.5-ounce / 100-g) bar semisweet chocolate, chopped

1 cup (120 g) unsweetened Hershey's Special Dark Cocoa

1 tablespoon (8 g) cornstarch

8 wedges blue cheese

PREP

Peel the pears. Slice a little bit off the bottom of the pears so that they are able to stand up on a plate without falling over. Then slice each pear in half vertically and scoop out the core. Put them in a bowl of water as you peel them to keep from browning.

COOK

Pears

Pour the whole bottle of wine into the French oven and add the vanilla, sugar, cinnamon stick, cloves, nutmeg, and blackberry jam. Bring to a boil over medium heat, reduce to a simmer, and cook for 3 minutes, whisking to combine. Lower the pears into the liquid, cover, and simmer for 20–30 minutes. The cooking time will vary depending on the ripeness and size of your pears. You want them to be firm but still tender when you pierce them. Take off the lid and leave the pears in the poaching liquid to cool to room temperature. Then cover and chill overnight.

The next day, transfer the pears and poaching liquid to a large bowl, removing and discarding the whole cloves.

continued >

Chocolate Sauce

Pour 1 cup (240 ml) of the poaching liquid into the French oven then add port wine, sugar, and rosemary and bring to a simmer, whisking to dissolve the sugar. Add the chocolate and cocoa and energetically whisk for a minute or so over the heat to dissolve. Mix the cornstarch with enough water to make a thin paste then whisk this mixture into the simmering wine for 3 minutes, or until the sauce has thickened.

To serve, you have the option of standing up 2 pear halves on each plate to make a whole pear, or standing up 1 half and slicing the other half and fanning the slices on each plate. Drizzle a little of the poaching liquid over the pears to moisten.

Swirl some of the chocolate sauce onto each plate and offer the rest in a pitcher or bowl. Stand a whole wedge of blue cheese next to the pears and serve.

IDEAS AND SUGGESTIONS

Use the leftover poaching liquid in your ice cream machine to make a super flavorful sorbet, adding a bit more sugar, to taste.

Make just the wine-poached pears and serve them on an antipasto platter with a selection of cheeses and sliced prosciutto.

HOT BRANDIED PEACHES OVER ICE CREAM

Pêches Chaudes au Brandy et Crème Glacée SERVES 6

One day at the post office, a woman in front of me was describing how she makes hot brandied peaches. I thought she meant canning spiced peaches then serving them warm. So I asked her how she made them, and she described the following process that produces a quick and really satisfying dessert that highlights fresh rather than canned peaches. I played around with the idea which resulted in the following recipe that's ready in no time.

SPECIAL EQUIPMENT 5.5-QUART (5.5-L) FRENCH OVEN

10 large ripe peaches

½ cup (120 ml) brandy, peach brandy, or apricot brandy, divided

1 stick (115 g) unsalted butter, room temperature

½ cup (90 g) light brown sugar

⅛ teaspoon ground cloves

2 teaspoons vanilla extract or seeds from 1 vanilla pod

½ teaspoon almond extract

¼ teaspoon ground cinnamon

2 quarts (2 l) ice cream

PREP

Prepare a large bowl of water with ice cubes and place it by the stove. Make an "X" with a small sharp knife on the bottom of each peach.

COOK

Add enough water to the French oven to be able to drop all the peaches in and bring to a boil over medium heat. Gently lower in the whole peaches and cook for only 30 seconds. With tongs or a slotted spoon, transfer the peaches to the ice water in the bowl. When they are cool, take them out, pat dry, and peel with a small sharp knife.

With a small sharp knife, slice into a peach, flesh to the pit, to score the peach. Keep doing this all the way around the peach so that you get 4 pieces. Then wiggle the pieces off the pit with the knife. Toss the pieces into a bowl. Repeat for all the peaches. Drizzle

peaches with ¼ cup (60 ml) brandy and stir to completely coat.

Empty the water from the French oven and wipe dry.

Melt the butter in the French oven over medium low heat. Add the brown sugar, ground cloves, vanilla extract, almond extract, and cinnamon. Bring to a simmer and let bubble for a minute or so while whisking.

Toss in the peaches, stir to coat, and cook for 5 minutes. Add the remaining brandy and stir well. Serve it hot and bubbly over ice cream.

IDEAS AND SUGGESTIONS

Use spiced rum, whiskey, white wine, coconut rum, Grand Marnier, or any of your favorite libations.

Garnish with chopped walnuts.

FRESH CHERRY SOUP WITH SUGAR COOKIES

Soupe de Cerises Fraîches et Biscuits Sablés SERVES 6

Chilled fruit soups are more common in Europe than in America, so at first this may seem an unusual dessert. It has a thin soup consistency, made from fresh cherries as they would in the Languedoc region of France.

I serve mine warm in large dessert bowls or parfait glasses with a scoop of vanilla ice cream melting in the center. I also make sugar cookies to serve with it as they go really well with this dessert. The recipe follows if you would like to make them.

SPECIAL EQUIPMENT 5-QUART (5-L) FRENCH OVEN

1 bottle dry red wine

¾ cup (150 g) sugar

1 stick cinnamon or ½ teaspoon ground cinnamon

¼ teaspoon almond extract

¼ teaspoon salt

2 teaspoons cornstarch dissolved in 2 tablespoons (30 ml) water

2½ pounds (1.2 kg) fresh dark cherries, pitted and sliced in half

¼ cup (60 ml) cherry brandy, Kirsch, or Guignolet cherry liquer, optional

Vanilla bean ice cream

COOK

Pour the wine into the French oven. Add the sugar, cinnamon, almond extract, and salt and bring to a boil. Whisk the cornstarch mixture into the wine, cooking until slightly thickened. Take off the heat, and cool to room temperature.

Strain the soup through a fine sieve placed over a large bowl. Discard contents in sieve. Pour the wine mixture from the bowl back into the French oven. Add the cherries and simmer for 2 minutes. If you are adding brandy or Kirsch, whisk it in.

Place a scoop of ice cream in each bowl or parfait glass, ladle in the warm soup and cherries, balance a cookie on top of each scoop of ice cream, and serve.

SUGAR COOKIES

MAKES 3 DOZEN 2½-INCH (6-CM) COOKIES

SPECIAL EQUIPMENT STAND MIXER; BAKING SHEETS

2¼ cups (270 g) all-purpose flour

½ teaspoon baking powder

½ teaspoon salt

¼ teaspoon cinnamon

2½ sticks (280 g) unsalted butter, room temperature

¾ cup (150 g) plus 2 tablespoons (30 g) granulated sugar

½ cup (100 g) light brown sugar

2 large eggs, beaten

½ teaspoon almond extract

1 teaspoon vanilla extract

PREP

Preheat oven to 350° F (180° C).

COOK

In a large bowl, sift together the flour, baking powder, salt, and cinnamon.

Using the stand mixer, beat the butter until fluffy. Add the sugars and beat again until fluffy. Add the eggs, almond extract, and vanilla extract and beat to just barely combine. Stir in the flour mixture.

Drop 1 level tablespoon of dough per cookie onto the baking sheets, about 2 inches (5 cm) apart. Wet your fingers and gently flatten the tops. They don't have to be perfect, just uniform in size. Bake for 15 minutes, until lightly browned around the edges. Cool and serve.

Note: If you would like small cookies, use a level teaspoon to drop the dough onto the baking sheets. The cookies will take 12 minutes to bake and will be 1½ to 2 inches (4 cm to 5 cm) wide. Super cute served with espresso.

IDEAS AND SUGGESTIONS

Add a dollop of whipped cream for the top. Or, try using a ruby port instead of red wine.

GARIGUETTE

JAMMING

For me, fresh jams are far superior to jams made to withstand months, if not years, on a shelf. And since I use mine up quickly anyway, or give overflow to neighbors, I do not have to make jams that require pectin or long sterilizing water baths.

This technique produces jewel-like colors and vibrant flavors. I love the spontaneity of scooping up beautiful fruit at farmers markets, knowing I can make jam with them in the morning for breakfast without more work or time involved that it takes to make pancakes.

These fresh jams are not highly set, and are more spreadable. Use your French oven for making them as the ovens are heavy and not likely to move while hot jam is bubbling away.

LUSCIOUS GREEN TOMATO AND LAVENDER JAM

Succulente Confiture de Tomate Verte et Lavande MAKES 6 TO 7 (8-OUNCE / 225-G) JARS

Made with hard green tomatoes, hard barely pink tomatoes, lavender, sugar, and lemon juice—this gooey sticky jam seems destined to be dolloped on top of a pillow of soft goat cheese on great bread or to be presented on a cheese board alongside cheeses with personality.

You begin by coating the tomatoes with lots of sugar, adding some fresh lavender blossoms or dried culinary lavender, and allowing it to sit for an hour or so for the juice from the tomatoes to flow to the bottom of the bowl.

Then you simmer them until all the liquid has bubbled away. Make sure to watch while they cook as the timing and the yield will vary depending on the ripeness of the tomatoes, the size you cut them, etc. For example, heirloom tomatoes will have a higher water content, on average, than Roma or standard tomatoes. You want to stop cooking when liquid bubbles have stopped appearing. When the jam is done, turn off the heat and stir for a couple of minutes to allow the last bit of moisture to evaporate.

SPECIAL EQUIPMENT 2 FRENCH OVENS, AS LARGE AS YOU HAVE; CANDY THERMOMETER; 6 TO 7 (8-OUNCE / 225-G) CANNING JARS

6 pounds (2.7 kg) green and pink hard unripe organic tomatoes	1 teaspoon kosher or sea salt	3 organic lemons, zested and juiced
9 cups (4 pounds / 1.8 kg) sugar	3 tablespoons fresh lavender blossoms or dried culinary lavender	1 tablespoon vanilla extract

COOK

Clean and pat dry the tomatoes then slice them into small chunks, keeping seeds, juice, and skin. Place into a large bowl and toss tomatoes with sugar, salt, and lavender.

After waiting at least an hour, divide between French ovens and bring to a boil over medium heat. Add the lemon juice, zest, and vanilla and stir.

Return to a boil over medium heat, reduce to a gentle simmer, and cook, stirring frequently, until all the liquid has evaporated and the tomato mixture is thick, or until the candy thermometer reads 212° F (100° C).

Ladle the jam into clean jars, cool to room temperature, then firmly tighten the lids and place in the refrigerator until ready to use.

IDEAS AND SUGGESTIONS

If you don't have access to lavender, substitute fresh thyme or minced fresh basil leaves.

FRESH STRAWBERRY JAM

Confiture de Fraises Fraîches MAKES 2 (8-OUNCE / 225-G) JARS

This recipe is for a small batch that is quick to make, taking anywhere from 15–45 minutes to thicken and doesn't need to go into a sterilizing bath. Just put it in the refrigerator. It will last for at least 2 weeks, if you don't use it up before then.

The riper the strawberries, the less pectin in them, so go for ones that are not overly ripe. Riper ones will have more juice and take longer for your jam to cook down. And as berries vary from region to region and from level of ripeness, timing until your jam thickens will vary. Use your instincts to guide you. I usually eyeball my jam and do the "plate in the freezer" test. When the liquid bubbles begin to disappear as the jam cooks, and I put a spoonful on a plate that was in the freezer and it gels, then I am pretty sure my jam has set.

SPECIAL EQUIPMENT 4.5-QUART (4.5-L) FRENCH OVEN OR LARGER

24 ounces (670 g) fresh
  strawberries

1 cup (200 g) sugar
½ large organic lemon, juiced

1 teaspoon vanilla extract

PREP

Rinse strawberries and pat very dry. Pull off stems and leaves. Put a small plate in the freezer, which you will use to test your jam.

COOK

Slice the strawberries into the French oven. Pour in the sugar. Add the lemon juice and vanilla extract.

Begin cooking over medium-low heat. When the fruit is warm, turn up the heat to medium so it simmers; stir frequently. As it cooks, you will see bubbles forming on the top. Keep stirring frequently and when you see no more bubbles forming, turn off the heat. At this point, the jam should be thick. To test it, take the plate out of the freezer and put a spoonful of jam on it. Wait 30 seconds. If it stays apart when you run your finger through it, it is done.

Let the jam cool for a few minutes then serve in a bowl. If you are using it later, ladle it into clean glass jars and let cool completely before covering and storing in the refrigerator.

FIG AND PORT CHUTNEY WITH CRUMBLY AGED CHEDDAR

Chutney de Figues au Porto, avec un Vieux Cheddar MAKES 6 CUPS (1.4 L)

My fig trees are long gone, so now I make jams and chutneys with dried figs and use them for more than spreading on toast. They are great in grilled cheese sandwiches, or thinned out with olive oil or port wine and brushed over a pork roast then served in a bowl with the sliced pork. I've swirled it into cheesecakes and smeared it between two cookies. And I store it in the refrigerator in a screw-top jar for up to 2 weeks.

You can make it in the afternoon and serve it that night with a lovely wedge of crumbly aged cheddar on crackers or country bread.

SPECIAL EQUIPMENT FRENCH OVEN 5-QUART (5-L) OR LARGER; FOOD PROCESSOR

24 to 28 ounces (670 to 780 g) dried Mission figs, coarsely chopped

1 cup (120 g) dried cherries

2 cups (480 ml) port wine, plus 3 tablespoons (45 ml), divided

½ cup (90 g) dark brown sugar

2 teaspoons Dijon mustard

¾ teaspoon ground cloves

1½ teaspoons salt

2 teaspoons dried rosemary or 1 tablespoon minced fresh rosemary

Large piece of crumbly aged cheddar cheese

Crackers or country bread

COOK

To the French oven, add the chopped figs, cherries, 2 cups (480 ml) port, brown sugar, mustard, cloves, salt, and rosemary. Cover, bring to a boil over medium heat, uncover, and reduce to a gentle simmer. Cook for about 6 minutes, until most of the liquid has evaporated and the figs are soft.

Turn off the heat and let the mixture rest for 12 minutes, stirring occasionally so that it cools. Transfer half of it to a food processor and purée until very

smooth. Scoop it back into the French oven and stir to combine. Stir in remaining port and mix well.

Serve on crackers with the cheddar over the top—or spoon into clean jars with screw-top lids and keep in the refrigerator or share with neighbors and friends.

IDEAS AND SUGGESTIONS

Instead of port, add rum and raisins. Instead of dried cherries, add in chopped oil-cured black olives.

DRINKS FOR A CROWD

I like for my parties to be fun and relaxing and include an interactive element where guests can help themselves to drinks prepared in and served from a French oven—especially in the colder months when you want something warm. As guests arrive, they are guided to the French oven on the stove where they can ladle their drink into a mug, while slowing down and making themselves comfortable in my kitchen. To continue the interactive theme, I often set up a food table or dessert buffet for guests to flow from the drink in the French oven to tasting food or trying out a bite of dessert, enjoying conversations along the way.

DO-IT-YOURSELF HOT CHOCOLATE BAR

Bar à Chocolat Chaud MAKES 14 CUPS

During the winter at my house in the hills in the south of France, I used to set up this hot chocolate bar on the wide stone ledge next to my fireplace. The fire would be crackling and copper pots gleaming as they hung above the dancing flames. As guests finished dinner and wandered into the living room, they would find this waiting for them. They could fill their cups then settle into my overly large white sofa and pillow-filled chairs to savor the warmth of the fire and the flavor of hot chocolate and Grand Marnier.

Because I lived in Bar-sur-Loup, the "village of oranges," I always made it with Grand Marnier, orange juice, and freshly grated orange zest, but you can take the basic recipe and add in any favorite liqueur and aromatics.

SPECIAL EQUIPMENT FOOD PROCESSOR; 5-QUART (5-L) OR LARGER FRENCH OVEN; MICROPLANE

3 (3.5-ounce / 100 g) bars bittersweet chocolate

1 small organic orange

2 teaspoons ground cinnamon

¾ cup (140 g) dark brown sugar, firmly packed

3 tablespoons (40 g) sugar

3 heaping tablespoons (20 g) instant espresso powder

13 cups (3 l) whole milk

2 teaspoons vanilla extract

1½ teaspoons almond extract

4 heaping tablespoons (40 g) Hershey's Special Dark Cocoa powder

1 cup (240 ml) Grand Marnier

Toppings

whipped cream

large chunk of white chocolate

bottle of Grand Marnier

marshmallows

cinnamon sticks

PREP

Coarsely break up chocolate. Zest and juice orange.

COOK

Toss broken chocolate, orange zest, cinnamon, brown sugar, sugar, and espresso powder into the food processor and pulse until chocolate is broken down. Then process until everything is finely chopped.

In the French oven, pour in the milk, vanilla extract, almond extract, and orange juice and cook over medium heat until it just begins to simmer. Scrape in the contents from the food processor, add the cocoa powder, and bring to a boil. Reduce to a simmer and whisk for about 3–5 minutes, until melted and thoroughly combined.

Whisk in the Grand Marnier. Taste, and add sugar or more Grand Marnier, if desired. Keep warm on the back burner on very low heat.

Set up the hot chocolate bar: Place a ladle to the side of the French oven. Have heatproof mugs arranged on the countertop. Next, place a bowl of whipped cream, a microplane with the chunk of white chocolate so guests can grate some on top of the whipped cream, an opened bottle of Grand Marnier for those who might like an extra splash in the bottom of their mug, a jar or bowl of marshmallows, and cinnamon sticks for stirring the drinks.

IDEAS AND SUGGESTIONS

Omit the Grand Marnier for an equally delicious alcohol-free version. For the holidays, serve with a bowl of candy canes for stirrers. Substitute peppermint schnapps and fresh mint leaves; spiced rum; Frangelico; or Kahlúa for the Grand Marnier.

HOLIDAY PARTY MULLED WINE

Vin Chaud des Fêtes de Noël MAKES 15 CUPS

I remember cold wet days in Paris where I would find refuge in a small café and order hot, spiced red wine, vin chaud. *And I remember days in the French Alps when I would come down from the mountain at the end of a day of skiing, park my skis and poles at the door to a restaurant in the village, and sit at outdoor tables sipping hot, spiced red wine to warm up. More than one glass will keep you very warm.*

Make it in a French oven on the stove for parties so that people can fill their own mugs. It fills the kitchen with a divine fragrance and will definitely put you and your guests in the holiday spirit having vin chaud at home.

SPECIAL EQUIPMENT 5.5-QUART (5.5-L) FRENCH OVEN

1 organic orange

1 organic lemon

½ cup (120 ml) water

¼ cup (50 g) sugar

¼ cup (50 g) light brown sugar

2 bottles red wine (inexpensive Merlot, Pinot Noir, Cabernet Sauvignon, Beaujolais Nouveau)

4 whole cloves

2 whole cinnamon sticks

2 star anise

½ teaspoon vanilla extract

½ cup (120 ml) cognac

2 cups (480 ml) ruby-red port

PREP

Zest and juice orange. With a vegetable peeler, peel the lemon then juice.

COOK

Pour the orange juice, lemon juice, water, and sugars into the French oven, bring to a boil, and whisk until the sugar dissolves.

Pour in the wine, and add the orange zest, cloves, cinnamon sticks, star anise, and vanilla. Partially cover and cook on a low simmer, do not boil, for 30 minutes. Pour in the cognac and port, stir, and taste.

Add more sugar, if needed, stirring and cooking until dissolved.

At the last minute add 4 lemon peels.

IDEAS AND SUGGESTIONS

Make black cherry mulled wine using 1 quart (1 l) black cherry juice to 2 bottles Cabernet Sauvignon with all the same ingredients, omitting the oranges. Try making it with white wine.

For an alcohol-free version, substitute grape juice or apple cider.

SNOWSTORM HOT RUM PUNCH

Punch Chaud au Rhum pour une Tempête de Neige Makes 15 cups

The chalet we had stopped in overnight was being pounded with snow, so much so that we booked another couple of nights to make sure we could get back on the road safely. That gave us a chance to get to know the owners and locals in the small bar in the lobby where everyone would gather to talk about their day and the weather. The bartender, the son of the owner, had spent a few years in sunny Bermuda and the Caribbean, so his drinks had a tropical twist that helped raise everyone's spirits. We were all stuck there, but it was his Hot Rum Punch that made us book for a return visit the next year. It is super easy to make at home. Just toss everything in a French oven and keep it on very low heat.

SPECIAL EQUIPMENT FOOD PROCESSOR; 5-QUART (5-L) OR LARGER FRENCH OVEN; MICROPLANE

2 Granny Smith apples

4 organic lemons

1 small organic orange

¾ cup (150 g) light brown sugar, tightly packed

½ teaspoon ground cloves

2 teaspoons ground cinnamon

2 teaspoons vanilla extract

12 cups (3 l) boiling water

1 bottle (750 ml) dark rum

1 whole nutmeg

Cinnamon sticks

PREP

Peel the apples, core, and thickly slice. Thickly slice 1 whole lemon. Squeeze remaining lemons. With a vegetable peeler, peel the orange then juice.

COOK

Toss the apple slices, sliced lemon, orange peel, brown sugar, cloves, cinnamon, and vanilla in the food processor and process until smooth.

Scoop into the French oven, add water and rum, and whisk to combine. Bring to a simmer and cook on low heat for 10 minutes. Keep warm on a back burner on very low heat.

To serve, have mugs set up nearby with a ladle to fill them with the punch. Place the microplane and whole nutmeg near the mugs to grate nutmeg on top of punch, if desired, and a bowl of cinnamon sticks to use as stirrers.

ACKNOWLEDGMENTS

I have an amazing team.

Steven Rothfeld is, to my mind, one of the best food photographers in the world today, and he has joined me yet again on this our third cookbook together. I am so very grateful for his dedication, suggestions, talent, and friendship. *Merci, mon ami.* Deborah Ritchken, my literary agent extraordinaire, is always there for me providing inspiration and friendship, as well as creating the stunning food styling for all three of my cookbooks. *Merci, Deborah.*

I have many volunteers who join me to work in the kitchen, to test recipes, to clean after all is done, and to taste test for me, providing commentary and suggestions as I develop recipes. Thanks to all of you, most especially to Beth Marinello, John Marinello, Stefan Ryll, Barbara Michelson, Sandy Taylor, Jen Cartmell, Jillian Bernardini, Betsy Slattery, Jane Cartmell, Susan Laughlin, the Fairfield Road taste testers, Blandine Hafela, Grove Hafela, and George Sheinberg. Special thanks to my friend and cookbook author, Hélène Lautier, for the French translations.

To my friends and social media followers who are virtually by my side every day encouraging me, providing moral support, and recipe testing for me. You know who you are and you know I am grateful for everything that you do.

To my publisher Gibbs Smith, my wonderful editor Michelle Branson, and her design team, my heartfelt thanks for creating another beautiful cookbook.

My sincere thanks go to the French manufacturers and artisans who furnished the props for the photo shoot, including the tablecloths, linens, dishes, cutlery, and French ovens: Zwilling J. A. Hencklels for providing Staub and Fontignac French ovens; French Home for providing Chasseur French ovens; Emile Henry for their French ovens; Le Creuset for their French ovens; Mauviel for their French ovens; Revol for their French ovens; Créations Jean-Vier for their Basque tablecloths, napkins, and dish towels; Jacquard Français for their tablecloths, place mats, and napkins; Garnier-Thibaut for their tablecloths; the French Farm for supplying us with Laguiole by Jean Dubost cutlery, olive wood steak knives, and serving pieces; La Rochere for "French Bee" glasses, wine glasses, and wine pitcher; Mottahedeh, Inc. for supplying us with JARS dinnerware from France; and Villa Cappelli in Italy for supplying us with all the olive oil we used for recipe testing.

And to Bill Cochrane, who graciously opened his home for my crew to be able to come together for the photo shoot for this book, who drove me late at night to food shop for the next day's photo shoot, and who always asked, "What can I do to help?"—my love always.

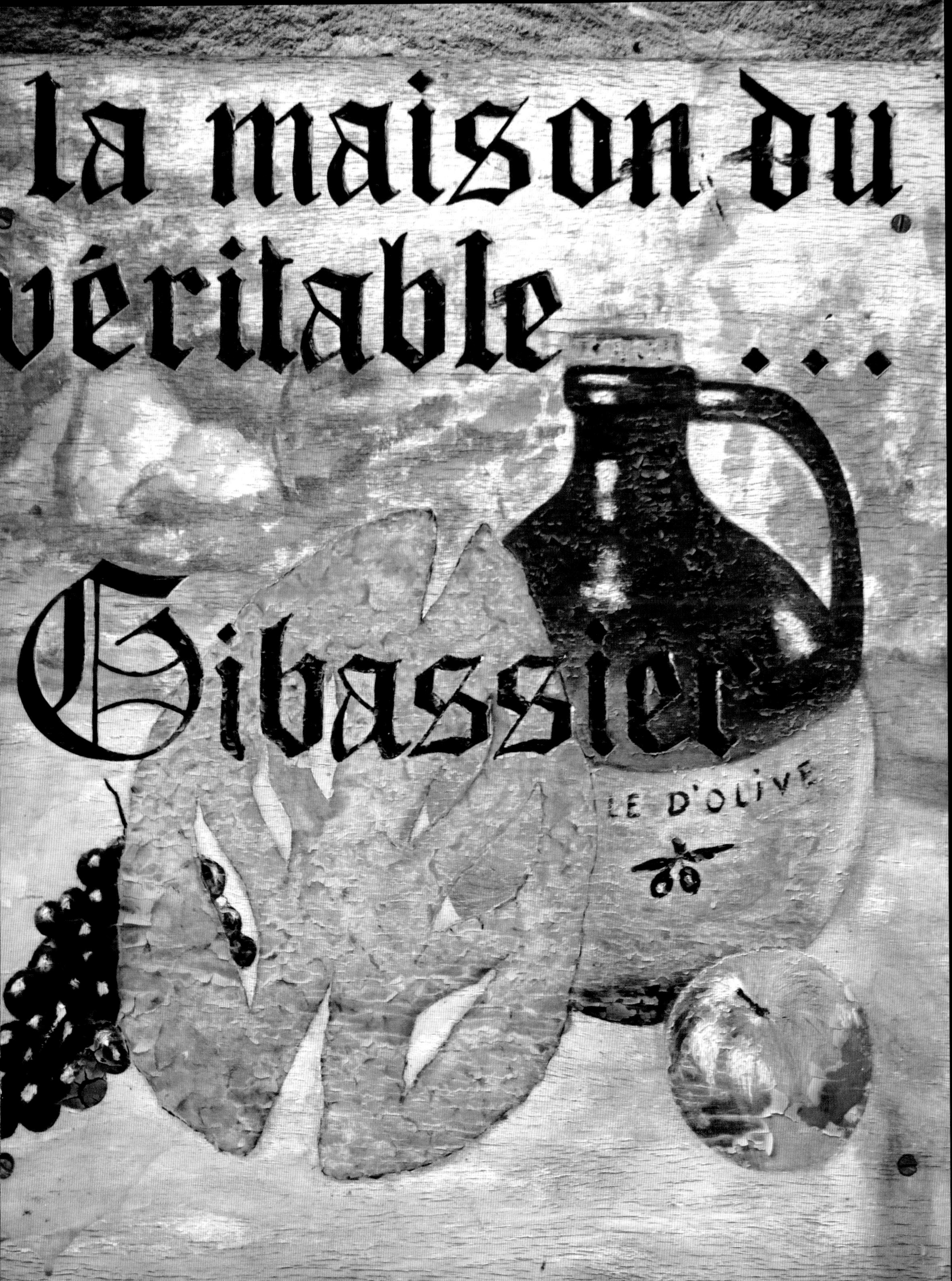
la maison du
véritable…
Gibassier
LE D'OLIVE

RESOURCES

FRENCH OVENS

Chasseur
U.S. Distributor:
French Home, LLC
94 Nickerson Road

Ashland, MA 01721

Telephone: 1-508-231-1189

Email: Michael@frenchhome.com

www.FrenchHome.com

Emile Henry
802 Centerpoint Blvd.

New Castle, DE 19720

Telephone: 1-302-326-4800

Email: ehoutletsales@emilehenryusa.com

www.emilehenryusa.com

www.facebook.com/pages/Emile-Henry/156176996545

Fontignac
Zwilling J. A. Henckels, Inc.

171 Saw Mill River Road

Hawthorne, NY 10532

Telephone: 1-800-777-4308

Email: zwillingonline@zwillingus.com

www.fontignac.com

www.facebook.com/

Le Creuset
114 Bob Gifford Blvd.

Early Branch, SC 29916

Telephone: 1-877-273-8738

Email: cservice@lecreuset.com

www.lecreuset.com

www.facebook.com/lecreuset

Mauviel USA Inc.
802 Centerpoint Blvd.

New Castle, DE 19720

Telephone: 1-302-326-4803

Email: info@mauvielusa.com

www.mauvielusa.com

www.facebook.com/pages/Mauviel-USA/280859390794

Revol USA
Brookside Court

4625 Alexander Drive, Suite 170

Alpharetta, GA 30022

Telephone: 1-678-456-8671

Email: info@revol-usa.com

www.revol-porcelaine.fr/en

www.facebook.com/Revol.USA

Staub
Zwilling J. A. Henckels USA

270 Marble Avenue

Pleasantville, NY 10570

Telephone: 1-800-777-4308

Email: infostaub@zwillingus.com

www.zwillingus.com

www.facebook.com/StaubUSA

FRENCH LINENS

Créations Jean-Vier

CD307

64310 Saint Pée sur Nivelle

France

Telephone: 1-33-(0)5-59-54-56-70

Email: info@jean-vier.com

www.jean-vier.com/en

www.facebook.com/creationsjeanvier

Garnier-Thiebaut Inc.

3000 S. Eads Street

Arlington, VA 22202

Telephone: 1-888-812-6670 x109

Email: info@gtlinens.com

www.gtlinens.com

www.facebook.com/GarnierThiebaut

Jacquard Français

31, rue Voltaire

92800 Puteaux

France

Telephone: 1-33-(0)3-29-60-09-04

www.le-jacquard-francaise.com

www.facebook.com/pages/

Mademoiselle-Jacquard/157637010945409

FRENCH CUTLERY

Laguiole by Jean Dubost

U.S. Distributor:

The French Farm

916b W. 23rd Street

Houston, TX 77008

Telephone: 1-713-660-0577

Email: gisele@frenchfarm.com

www.frenchfarm.com

FRENCH GLASSWARE

La Rochere North America Inc.

65 Pondfield Road

Bronxville, NY 10708

Telephone: 1-914-337-1081

Email: info@larochere.com

www.larochere.com

FRENCH DINNERWARE

Jars France

Mottahedeh, Inc.

5 Corporate Drive

Cranbury, NJ 08512

Telephone: 1-800-443-8225

Email: customerservice@mottahedeh.com

www.mottahedeh.com

www.facebook.com/MottahedehFineChina

ITALIAN OLIVE OIL

This is my house olive oil, made by my friend, Paul Cappelli.

Villa Cappelli

Via Appia Traiana, 11

Terlizzi (BA) 70038

Italy

Email: info@villacappelli.com

www.shop.villacappelli.com

www.facebook.com/VillaCappelli

INDEX

ABOUT THE AUTHOR

Hillary Davis is the author of *Le French Oven*, *French Comfort Food*, *Cuisine Niçoise: Sun-Kissed Cooking from the French Riviera*, and the critically acclaimed book, *A Million A Minute*.

Her passion for France and French food propelled her to move to the tiny village of Bar-sur-Loup in the south of France, where she learned to how cook local dishes from women and friends in the village during the eleven years she lived there. As a result, she provided private cooking classes and catering for Americans living along the Riviera.

An authority on French cuisine as well as a longtime food writer and restaurant critic, she is also a cooking instructor, frequently lectures on the topic of food, is a judge of cooking competitions, a speaker at food events, a food and travel lecturer on Royal Caribbean and Celebrity cruise lines, and is a frequent guest on television and radio programs. As a food journalist, her work has been featured in *French Entrée Magazine*, *Bonjour Paris*, *Tastes of New England*, *Connecticut Living*, *Hartford Magazine*, *New Hampshire Magazine*, ParisLuxe.com, eGuideTravel.com, and other regional and international publications as well as on her popular food blog, Marche Dimanché.

She holds a degree in economics from Columbia University and a Masters in International Relations from Cambridge University. Please visit www.Hillary-Davis.com.

Steven Rothfeld is a world-class photographer specializing in luxury imagery. His book credits include *The Tuscan Sun Cookbook*, *Bringing Tuscany Home*, *Simply French*, *In the Shade of the Vines*, *Entrez*, *The French Cook—Sauces*, *Hungry for France*, *Cuisine Niçoise*, and *French Comfort Food*. He divides his time between destinations throughout the world and his home in Napa Valley. Please visit www.stevenrothfeld.com.